BITTEN BY THE
BLACK SNAKE

The Ancient Wisdom of Ashtavakra

SENTIENT PUBLICATIONS

First Sentient Publications edition 2007
Copyright © 2007 by Manuel Schoch

A paperback original

Cover design by Kim Johansen, Black Dog Design
Book design by Linda Harper, Harper Design

Library of Congress Cataloging-in-Publication Data

Schoch, Manuel, 1946-
[Tao des Gl I cks. English]
Bitten by the black snake : the ancient wisdom of Ashtavakra / Manuel Schoch.
p. cm.
ISBN 978-1-59181-060-5
1. Astavakragita—Criticism, interpretation, etc. 2. Advaita. 3.
Spiritual life—Hinduism. I. Title.

132.A3S4413 2007
181'.482—dc22
2007013427

Printed in the United States of America

10 9 8 7 6 5 4 3 2 1

SENTIENT PUBLICATIONS

A Limited Liability Company
1113 Spruce Street
Boulder, CO 80302
www.sentientpublications.com

CONTENTS

Contents

CONTENTS

FOREWORD

A SUTRA IS LITERALLY A THREAD. SUTRAS ARE BARE THREADS of exposition unadorned by excesses, because of course they were delivered at a time before books existed and so had to be tersely expressed.

This book is unique in that it relates Ashtavakra's sutras to a modern context. Although Ashtavkra predates Jesus Christ, Mohammed, and perhaps Buddha, his wisdom chimes with that of contemporary masters.

Little is known about the author of these sutras, which are thought to originate from the 4th or 5th century BC. It is said that Ashtavakra was the son of a lesser disciple of the great sage Uddalaka, married to Uddalaka's daughter. The unborn child, who already had mastered the Vedas, kept twisting and turning within the womb, unable to bear his father's mistakes in recitation, and was therefore born with eight deformations. Hence he was called Ashta (eight) Vakra (bends). Ashtavakra went on to become a great sage himself, and had the honor of having the king as one of his students.

These sutras are meant to reflect a dialogue between Ashtavakra and King Janaka on the nature of the soul, reality, and bondage and the means to liberation. Ancient teachers would repeat a sutra by heart and then go on to amplify it for the benefit of their pupils. Here, Manuel Schoch is amplifying Ashtavakra's sutras, and helping the reader get into the very consciousness of Ashtavakra.

Manuel's reflections put us at the crossroads between psychology and spirituality — that point of combustion that can deliver us to another dimension of higher spiritual integration, beyond the ego. Like Ashtavakra's, Manuel's insights are direct and penetrating, leaving little leeway for misinterpretation. In reading these words it becomes apparent that both Manuel and Ashtavakra are masters in dealing with the mind.

In Manuel's discussion of the sutras, the age old issues of fear, desire, feelings, and stillness are grappled with skilfully. Manuel crisscrosses his deep exposition with references to his own Time Therapy and to other major philosophical systems.

It is refreshing to hear Manuel reinforce Ashtavakra's observation that being at peace with everything is key to attaining enlightenment and how this doesn't involve changing a single thing about oneself. Read on and be enlightened.

—Dr. Adeline Wright

THE FIRST SUTRA

*Janaka asked, "Oh Lord, how does one attain
liberation and how is non-attachment attained? Please tell me this."*

*Ashtavakra replied, "Oh beloved, if you want liberation, then
renounce the passions as poison and take forgiveness and innocence,
compassion, contentment, and truth as nectar.*

You are neither earth nor air nor fire nor water nor ether.

*To attain liberation know yourself as the witnessing consciousness
of all these. If you separate yourself from the physical body and
rest in consciousness then this very moment you will be happy,
at peace, and free of bondage.*

*You are not a Brahmin or other caste. You are not in any of the
four stages of life.*

You are not perceived by the eyes or other senses.

*Unattached and without form, you are the witness of the
whole universe.*

Know this and be happy.

*Oh expansive one, religion and atheism, happiness and misery,
order of the mind – they are not for you.*

You are neither the doer nor the enjoyer.

You have always been liberated."

THE WISDOM OF THIS SUTRA IS THAT IT URGES YOU TO SEE
yourself as the witness or the observer. The heart of the sutra
has a simplicity and directness that cannot be found elsewhere
in Hinduism or in Buddhism.

Ashtavakra's wisdom penetrates deeper than any other because his sword of wisdom cuts directly to the root of consciousness. His teachings tell us that every form of existence, including religion itself, should not be taken seriously. He may have lived before the time of the Buddha, but had they been contemporaries, Ashtavakra would not have followed the Buddha's teachings.

Ashtavakra tells us that we are constantly accepting the form of the body as a fact. He does not say, however, that the body is *not* a fact. In this sutra, he is urging you to see that you are much more than just the body. You are consciousness – beyond the body, beyond the existence of form.

THE WITNESSING CONSCIOUSNESS

How does Ashtavakra arrive at this understanding? What does he mean when he says that if you want to be happy you have to see beyond form? He is encouraging you to see that you are the observer or, in his words, the witnessing consciousness.

Imagine that you are in a pitch dark room full of objects – plants, pictures, chairs, tables, paintings, a TV, and so on – and your eyes are closed. Now imagine that you open your eyes, and they shine like two flashlights; suddenly, whatever the flashlights shine on becomes visible. This is consciousness. Consciousness is you being the light. When this light is focused on objects, you can see them.

This does not mean (as some philosophers later claimed) that nothing exists without your consciousness. This is nonsense. For example, a tree exists even if there is no human consciousness observing it. You cannot see the tree, however, if you are not focusing the light on it – if you are not "being" the light.

So we can all shine like a flashlight if we open the eyes of consciousness. When we are witnessing, we create light in order to see. Without the witness, or the observer, things are there, but there is no consciousness of them. Whatever you are aware of exists because you are light. A dead body may have its eyes open, but it will not see anything, because there is no light, no consciousness.

Ashtavakra says simply that the basis of all wisdom is the observer. Everything else is an illusion – not because it doesn't exist, but because its reality is just like a dream. While you are dreaming you are very conscious of what's going on in the dream. You are convinced that what you are dreaming is really happening. If you dream that a lion is chasing you, in the dream you will try to escape from it. Upon waking up, you realize that there was no lion chasing you and your fear was based on an illusion.

Ashtavakra asks us to imagine what it would be like to wake up in the middle of such a dream, turn around, and command the lion to stop. The lion would disappear. But we cannot do this in dreams, let alone in daily life. Nevertheless, Ashtavakra tell us that we are nothing other than the observer, and until we realize that, we can never obtain liberation.

THE DOER AND THE OBSERVER

If this is true, if I am really the observer, then I cannot be the doer. The doer is therefore the mind. This presents a great deal of confusion. In Zen, for example, there is the notion of *neti neti* and *wu wei* – the doing in not doing. There is also the saying that once you are enlightened, every action is a good one. This creates confusion if you think of the doer as the source of action directed toward the outside world.

Ashtavakra says that action resides in the mind, and modern science confirms this precisely. Action starts in the inner world of the mind. Modern science tells us that there is no difference in your brain activity whether you slap someone or merely think of slapping someone, for example. In the brain's limbic system, which is where motor control is expressed, just thinking of slapping someone activates all the muscles that would be used to do it.

We are reminded here of Jesus' teaching that if you just think of being unfaithful to your wife you have committed a sin. Once you take morality out of the equation, you can truly appreciate the depth of this wisdom.

The brain and everything the mind imagines is the action element of doing. However, if one is the observer, this observer is more than the mind, more than the doer.

Whenever you are taking any action, either in your mind or of a physical nature, you are not in a state of observation. Hence no liberation. Ashtavakra goes even deeper and calls this state "witnessing consciousness." He doesn't say just witness or observe; he calls it witnessing consciousness.

Witnessing consciousness means the observer *is* consciousness, not that the observer is separated from consciousness. Now recognizing this has a very deep impact. The observer is consciousness, so being connected to the observer provides liberation from the doer or liberation from the mind. Whenever the mind is without observation, then there is no consciousness.

It follows logically that if everything is consciousness, then there is nothing to aim for, nothing to gain, nothing to understand. If you are consciousness, you cannot be more than consciousness itself. Now, this is tremendously important to understand – not in the sense of intellectually grasping the idea of it, but in the sense of feeling, of seeing it.

GETTING IN THE WAY OF LIBERATION

In answer to the question "How can I obtain happiness or liberation?" Ashtavakra replies that liberation *is* being consciousness. He says that from the very beginning you are consciousness, and therefore you are liberated. It is the doing – the action of the mind – that gets in the way of liberation.

Doing is expressed in the form of the observer wanting to

reach some distant goal, and this creates a prison for the mind. The desire to be consciousness is precisely the barrier to enlightenment. If there is only consciousness, then enlightenment is part of consciousness, therefore there is no need to reach out for enlightenment. You cannot, says Ashtavakra, become better or worse.

"You are not identified with the four stages of life. You are not perceived by the eyes or senses," Ashtavakra says. Of course you need your eyes and the other senses to function in life, but you are more than this. You can see and feel in consciousness without the body senses. Ashtavakra says liberation is the art of being unattached to all this – a state of being in which you are the witness of the whole universe.

In fact, at the heart of his teachings Ashtavakra is saying that each movement of doing – each effort you make to become better, to get more wisdom, or to achieve your goals – is bound to fail because it is a barrier to consciousness. If you *are* consciousness and consciousness is shown in the observer, then trying to achieve something only limits consciousness.

Returning to the dark room metaphor, whenever you focus with your mind on something, the light goes off, and the room becomes dark. Then you decide that you need light to see things, and you try even harder to shed some light, but in doing so you create even more darkness. Ashtavakra tells you to just relax to attain liberation, to know yourself. What does he mean by this?

GAMES OF THE MIND

"Know yourself" means just relax and see that you are the witnessing consciousness. Don't try to know yourself for your strengths or weaknesses, your good or bad points, your tendencies or habits. Just know yourself as the witnessing consciousness. Then, of course, the mind will immediately want to know how to do this. It is the nature of the mind to ask this question.

In a later sutra Ashtavakra says that as long as you ask the question of how to achieve the state of witnessing consciousness, you have not grasped what it is to be the witnessing consciousness. The question *how* immediately creates a barrier. The mind needs concepts, theoretical structures, ideas, pictures, and religions. The *how* is the desperate attempt of the mind to keep itself alive.

The question *how* does nothing more than nourish desire. You may believe in Buddhism because you desire to become enlightened, or in Christianity because there is a deep desire to become a good person like Jesus. You want to be good because deep inside you is a desire not only to be good but also to be special.

Ashtavakra says that all this doing and action are the games of the mind. The root of misery, he says, is desire. The desire might be superficial or materialistic. For example, you may want to have a bigger house, or aim for self-improvement to become a better person, or try to rid of yourself of a weakness or problem, or you might desire enlightenment.

Ashtavakra says that the only way not to fall into that trap of desire is to separate from body consciousness. This makes Ashtavakra's wisdom sound so modern.

DESIRE FOR ENLIGHTENMENT

In the last ten years modern science has found that there is no separation between body and mind – that they are one and the same. When Ashtavakra talks about the body, he also includes the brain and the mind. The brain creates the mind. There is no mind without the brain.

What I call *out-of-the-body consciousness* is different from our experience of normal consciousness in our daily lives, which I call *body consciousness,* meaning the ordinary senses and the feedback they give us. The ordinary observer can be there only because there is a body. This form of consciousness is simply an electrochemical discharge of the brain, so without a brain it does not exist.

When Ashtavakra advises separation from the body, he does not just mean body as flesh and muscle, he means the mind, which is the "I," the ego. He says that only when you see yourself as separate from your body-mind can you rest in consciousness, and in that very moment you will be happy, at peace, and free of bondage.

But here comes the bind. Who is going to be happy when you have separated from the body? Who is going to be conscious about happiness when *you* are consciousness? Who is going to observe happiness when the observer is no longer observing something, but when the observer and the observed are in fact one?

Ashtavakra says once you have disconnected from the body-mind you will be happy, but later he tells us that, sadly, you will not be aware that you are happy because you will not be concerned with such a question.

Let me put it this way. If you think you are enlightened and you ask the question "Am I enlightened?" then you have not understood what enlightenment is. Once you are enlightened you won't be concerned about the question of enlightenment. You won't even know that you are enlightened.

This is because the root of misery is desire. And desire can be present only because one has not separated from the body-mind. Having desire indicates that one still hasn't really understood, because enlightenment can be present only when there is not a trace of desire. This observation is what makes Ashtavakra so clever. Listen to what he is saying, how he uses each word very consciously. He is not asking you to do anything, for example to separate from the body, and he is not saying that after doing this you will then be happy. No, he says rest in consciousness, and in this very movement you will be happy.

A STATE OF HAPPINESS

Have you ever been able to have a feeling, a sensation, an understanding, or a reflection when you are fully engaged in the present? Impossible. Have you ever thought about exactly what is happening when you are in the present – in the so called now? Now is not the absence of time. Time is a concept involving past and future. But what is really happening in what we call the now? In my observation (which is, of course, limited to my consciousness), only two things can happen. You can either move toward making a decision or toward stillness. The movement of decision brings you into awareness, the realization of things. The movement of stillness is pure consciousness.

Ashtavakra says there is stillness in separating from the body-mind. Any reflection that you might have about being happy can only follow stillness, once the stillness is gone. Have you observed yourself when you are really happy – not just because you are experiencing pleasure or enjoying something, but happy in the sense of being in samadhi, purely in a state of happiness – relaxed, resting in consciousness? In this state there is no need to do anything. Happiness is in fact the state where you stop wanting to be something. The desire is gone.

It is worth repeating that there is absolutely no possibility of being in a state of happiness as long as there is any trace of desire. Desire creates the need for action and initiates the movement toward misery. The movement might be toward decisions that have to be made in life. These decisions should never be made out of action and desire, but always out of stillness, where there is no sense of feeling good or special, or being aware of peace or happiness. The mind will revolt and insist on wanting to feel these things. As we all know, feeling good eventually disappears. You can feel beautiful one day, but if stillness doesn't follow, then by the next day the beauty evaporates.

Most of us can easily experience feeling good several times a day. But all things must pass, and therefore all these good feelings must end. That's why Ashtavakra says, "Religion and atheism, happiness and misery are all of the mind." All of the successes one can achieve are nothing other than achievements of the mind.

BEHIND THE MASK

Happiness, misery, or success – it's all in the mind. Ashtavakra is not admonishing you for enjoying happiness and success – he simply reminds you that this will not bring about true liberation. He is not against pleasure or enjoyment, but he says don't fool yourself and think of this as liberation. If you have five million dollars you will definitely have an easier life than someone who has to fight for survival every day, but this will not make you truly liberated.

You may be lucky, you may have a beautiful family, you may be loved, you may have physical and mental health, but Ashtavakra says even then, don't be fooled – this is not liberation. You may even play the part of the guru, the enlightened one, but don't fool yourself – this is not liberation.

This morning I was listening to sounds from the carnival celebration outside when I thought of an image that will help you to understand consciousness. Imagine that every year for the past six years you have gone to the carnival dressed in different costumes. For example, once you went dressed as a clown, then as a witch, and the following year as an angel, and so on. Now you have six years' worth of photos of yourself in carnival masks and carnival clothes. You present these photos to me, asking if I recognize these people. Of course I will say no, until I realize that behind the different masks and clothes is the same person.

Whatever role you play in this life, what lies beyond the role is always consciousness. Whenever a person appears in front of you claiming to have changed, to be wiser, to be better, be aware that this is so utterly unimportant. Behind the mask, behind the carnival of life, there is always the same consciousness.

One day someone is against you, the next day they are for you, another day they may have something critical to say about you. Behind the mask of being against or for you, of admiring or hating you, there is always consciousness. There are not six different people going to the carnival over the six years. The most important thing is that it is always exactly the same consciousness. The same applies to you and your consciousness.

Don't make issues about superficial levels or appearances. Ashtavakra tells us that fancy ideas, wonderful feelings about spirits and gods, or mystical experiences are not liberation. And why are they not liberation?

Here again we can see the depth of wisdom in these sutras. Challenging the beliefs of his time about a person's age, status, and achievement, or whether they could be identified with the elements of earth, fire, air, and water, Ashtavakra cuts through all of this. He says, "You are not any of the four stages of life. You are not perceived by the eyes or other senses.

Therefore as you are not these, and only when you are unattached and without form [which means separated from the body-mind], only then are you the witness of the whole universe."

This means that you are the witness not just of certain things, but of the whole universe. Enlightenment is not separated from the universe, and this is why Jesus claimed, "I am God." This is why Mohammad said, "I and Allah are one." There is no separation between the universe and consciousness. I am the consciousness in the universe. I am the universe.

FREE WILL

So what exactly is Ashtavakra trying to tell us? He uses the word *unattached*. There has been much confusion about the meaning of *unattached*. It doesn't mean that you no longer have a commitment to something, that you are detached; this misunderstanding is a product of the confusion of the mind, the doer.

What Ashtavakra is saying has nothing to do with this kind of superficial detachment. He is going much deeper. He says that being unattached is having free will. To be attached means there is no free will. From attachment to dependency there is but a tiny movement, only one degree of difference. So then we have to ask, what is free will?

Ashtavakra explains this in one of the later sutras connected with desire. Remember, he says that misery starts with desire. Desire creates action. Desire is the barrier to consciousness and when there is desire, one has the illusion of free will, but there is no real free will. As modern science has shown, before you even think about moving your finger there is a buildup of ready potential in the brain – i.e., no free will. So Ashtavakra says attachment is the process of having no free will.

We are under the illusion that in having the freedom to act, we are exercising our free will, but Ashtavakra says this is always an impulse activated from the outside. (Remember, action is always a synonym for the mind in Ashtavakra's philosophy.) Would you have the desire to be enlightened if there were no active patterns from the outside indicating how you should be? Is any action possible out of your own free will? Could he be right in saying that as all our impulses originate from outside influences, when action does arise, there is no free will?

MODERN MEDITATION

It is medically and scientifically proven that when there is a sensation in your body, let's say a tingling in your finger, it takes half a second before it is perceived in your brain. Therefore, there is a delay between the stimulus in your finger and the registration of consciousness of it – a gap of half a second, which we will call space. This gap is where the possibility of free will resides. Let's say that somewhere in your finger there is a little pain. The illusion is that this pain is happening right now. In reality it happened half a second ago, but your brain has taken that long to register it. By the time you register the pain in your brain, the finger may already be free of pain. What usually happens is that in this half second you immediately react and therefore there is never space, or what Ashtavakra calls free will.

In what Time Therapy calls Modern Meditation, we can observe that between each stimulus and the reaction, there is space. If you can observe the space and not react to the impulse, you have exercised free will. In the words of the Buddha or Ashtavakra, this would be detachment. In other words, free will arises when you cease to react to an impulse.

When Ashtavakra says, "You are not perceived by the eyes or senses," he means that if you can observe the space and not react to what is coming toward you from the outside – no matter what is happening with each impulse on the body level, or on the thought or feeling level – you will naturally separate from the body-mind. You will be free of desire, and this is what is meant by liberation.

THE SPACE OF STILLNESS

You cannot arrive at stillness by trying not to have thoughts or sensations in the body or feelings. This would simply lead to repression, not stillness. Stillness arises in the space between the impulse and the action. This is what Ashtavakra means by consciousness.

Consciousness is not an awareness of sensation, thought, or feeling. It is about being conscious of that which is in between forms. Ashtavakra says that forms are an illusion. A sensation is a form. A thought is a form. Observe that whenever you have a thought, it creates a picture. Whenever you bring action into the picture, you manifest a form. Each feeling is a form. It may not have a form manifested as an object, but it is a subjective form. Consciousness is that which is in between the forms.

In the words of the Zen masters, "The waves are the forms, and the whole ocean is that which is in between the waves." The waves are form; they appear and vanish. This applies to everything that exists that is part of consciousness, whether it is a hundredth-of-a-millisecond of a form or a form that's eighty years old. Form stays form and will at some point have to fade away, returning to the ocean of consciousness.

Just a few days ago I saw a beautiful documentary on TV about evolution, the development from different animals to human beings. The film ended with the words, "Please remember, no species has survived forever." If the dinosaurs had not died out, human life may not have existed, and one day we too will have to make way for a different species. The idea that human beings are at the top of the evolutionary chain is ridiculous. We are a form too, bound to vanish one day.

So Ashtavakra says don't cling to the form. Be consciousness. Consciousness is about watching the space, not being in the illusion that we have free will. In the words of Christ, this means faith and trust. Jesus says that God's will can be done only when you are no longer concerned with your form. This is the paradox – we have to stop identifying with and depending on form. It is the illusion of free will, the idea that we can do something instead of becoming part of consciousness.

To return to our metaphor, imagine that you are in a very dark room. You are a metaphor for light – you become light when your eyes are open. When you open your eyes you "wake up," so to speak. At first, when you are in this room and you open your eyes, you will focus on certain things that you can see – for example, a picture, a plant, a window. This is still form. The next step would be to realize that the goal is not to open your eyes in order to see, but to just open your eyes so that there is light in the room. Just allow there to be light without trying to do or see anything. Here, then, there is no desire, therefore no purpose, no motivation behind it. Who needs free will in this moment?

PERCEIVING WITH THE SENSES

Look at the beauty of this. First you open your eyes because you want to see. You, being light, are using the light to perceive. This is Ashtavakra's reference to "first the senses, the body, the mind." Then there is a shift in understanding accompanied by the dropping out of the body-mind, i.e., detachment. The understanding here is that you are pure consciousness. So now you do not open your eyes conscious that you are light and you will use this light to see – instead, the understanding is just that you are light and there is light. There is no more action directed toward something, no more purpose – just light, consciousness. Ashtavakra says, in this there is liberation with nothing to do, nothing to achieve, nothing to understand. Not focusing on any particular thing in the room, but instead just being light.

LIGHT VS. RELIGION

It may be that there are forms that would benefit from you being just light, just consciousness, but Ashtavakra says, why bother about this? If your motivation for enlightenment is that you will be able to help other people, it will not happen, and if it does seem to be happening, it will just become another religion.

Ashtavakra was so clear and precise in cutting through to the root of consciousness that he left no space for any interpretation that could be used to develop a religious system. Religious systems occur only when there is plenty of space for interpretation of the original text of the exponent of the religion.

You cannot have philosophical discussions about what Ashtavakra is saying. It is very clear and down to earth and therefore it's impossible to create a belief system or religion around it. This is the way things are, he says, so who is the doer and who is the one who enjoys or benefits from liberation? If you already are liberated, what's the fun in enjoying liberation? If you have always been enlightened, what's the need in saying you are liberated, or enlightened? If you have always been enlightened, you simply cannot investigate whether or not you are enlightened.

For instance, you don't celebrate the act of waking up from sleep every morning! The same goes for the state of being asleep. And this is an even better example: you don't think every night about how amazing it would be to be able to fall asleep. If you did, you would have great difficulty in falling asleep. "Rest in consciousness," says Ashtavakra. Don't make a fuss about the form. Without this, there can be no liberation.

CONSCIOUSNESS AND HEART ENERGY

We now understand how each action is a barrier to enlightenment. Action arises out of desire. Desire, in turn, is created by impulses. In reply to the question "How can I be happy and liberated?" Ashtavakra says rest in consciousness: that's fulfilllment, that's happiness, that's enlightenment. To rest in consciousness is what I call a state of stillness of the heart.

And he says know yourself as the witnessing consciousness of all this. In other words, he means be the observer. Ashtavakra says that to *be* consciousness requires observation and separation from the body. When we talk of the body, we include body consciousness, thoughts, feelings, and sensations, all of which are triggered in the brain. The witnessing consciousness, the observation he is talking about, is not taking place in the brain. If it were, it would not be possible to *be* consciousness, to be observing all of this. Time Therapy calls this out-of-body consciousness. Out-of-body consciousness must however be located somewhere and must somehow be connected to the physical body.

STILLNESS OF THE HEART

The place of connection, or the anchor of out-of-body

consciousness, is the heart and the heart energy. The heart energy, if you imagine a cross, is that meeting point of the vertical and the horizontal, of today and tomorrow, the past and the future – the meeting point between different dimensions. Heart energy is a point where there is either decision or stillness.

It is often said that the quality of courage, for instance, arises out of the heart, not the mind – otherwise it cannot be courage. Modern science will confirm that it is impossible to make a decision without feelings. It is the heart that brings together thought and feelings, and it can also deal with different dimensions, different time structures. The heart makes it possible to find a balance between body consciousness and out-of-body consciousness. This is what I call the stillness of the heart.

When you are in this state of stillness, you do not have the feeling that anything special is happening. This is why stillness and being with the heart go together. Later on you might reflect about the beauty and the happiness of the experience, but at the precise moment of that crossing point at the level of the heart there is only the making of decisions, and the movement toward something or stillness.

Ashtavakra says "Know yourself as the witnessing consciousness of all this – the forgiveness, the innocence, the compassion, the contentment, the truth." He says know yourself, but if you try to remember that with mind consciousness then you are in a state of action. So remembering the connection to the stillness of the heart is the remembrance of "knowing yourself." This is how it works.

You, the reader of this book, are sitting here and you are breathing. Where do you really breathe from? There are various ways of perceiving breathing. In classical meditation we might be advised to breathe deeply from the *hara* center, or in Vipassana, for example, to just watch the movement of the breath.

We realize that breathing happens through the mouth or the nose or both, but there is another breathing center at the anchor, located at the place of the physical heart and the heart center. The way to get in touch with the attitude of knowing yourself – realizing that you are nothing other than the observer – is by breathing at the level of the heart. To do this, simply shift your awareness to the level of the heart energy and just breathe in from the heart and breathe out from the heart.

In Modern Meditation this is called cultivating the stillness of the heart. In Ashtavakra's words it would be remembering, or knowing yourself constantly as nothing other than the witnessing consciousness – the witness of the whole universe.

When you begin to breathe in and out from the heart while maintaining the attitude of knowing yourself, of being the observer, then the space between impulse and action lengthens. If you have a sharp pain in your knee, you can increase the time between impulse and perception to more than half a second by breathing in and out from the heart over and over again.

This means that instead of reacting to the pain, you rest in the space between the impulse and the action, and this is what the mystics call emptiness, stillness, God. The word God, when applied correctly, is never used in relation to forms; it is always about that which occurs in that space and that stillness. Consciousness is not about form. The form becomes part of consciousness. Consciousness *is* that space. So to know yourself, just breathe in and out with your heart energy.

The beauty of the wisdom of Ashtavakra – and let's be very clear about this – is that meditation is also a movement of doing. Ashtavakra does not ask you to refrain from doing anything, because if you do nothing you become passive. He does not, for example, tell you not to meditate. Meditation may help you to cultivate stillness of the heart, but remember that meditation is still a process of doing and therefore not, in itself, consciousness. Be aware that meditation, too, is a form.

THE SECOND SUTRA

*You are the one observer of all and in reality
always free.*

*Your bondage is this – you see the other, not yourself, as the observer
and the doer; thus has the black snake of ego bitten you.*

I am not the doer.

Drink this divine nectar of fruit and be happy.

*I am the one pure awareness, thus I have burnt the forest of your
ignorance with this fire of certainty.*

Being beyond sorrow, be happy.

*You are that bliss, that ultimate bliss within which this imaginary
world is projected, like a snake and a rope.*

Knowing this, wonder happily.

*He who considers himself free is free, and he who considers himself
bound is bound, because in this world the proverb is true,
"As you think, so you are."*

*The soul is the witness, all pervading one, free consciousness; free
from doing, absolutely alone, non-attached, desireless, peaceful.*

Because of illusion it looks like the world.

I am an individually projected life.

*Drop this illusion and also this feeling of inner and outer, and
awaken in the thought that you are the unchanging, conscious,
and non-dual soul.*

THE SECOND SUTRA BEGINS WITH THE MESSAGE THAT
Ashtavakra offers repeatedly in every sutra. You are the
observer, not the form, not the ideas, not the doer. Then he goes

to a depth not reached by Mohammad, Buddha, or Jesus. Ashtavakra does not say only, "You are observation," he goes on to say, "You are the one observer."

This clears up a common misunderstanding about observation. He says that the bondage we create for ourselves involves seeing the other, not yourself, as the observer. Let's look at the depth of this.

LOOKING OUT, LOOKING IN

Ashtavakra says that when you confuse the art of observation by observing others, that is, focusing on what's happening outside of yourself, you are not truly observing the one observer. What you are doing is mirroring what you see outside, back into your brain. The art of observation is when you start to look outside by constantly observing yourself. The forms outside yourself – other people, objects, and things – are not the important objects to observe.

In Zen it is often said, "Look at the tree, become one with the tree." Ashtavakra tells us not to focus on nature or on any beautiful object – this is not observation. Observation is about constantly observing what is happening inside. Meditation is the movement inside, not outside. Even if the outside is real, you have to imagine that it is an illusion. Not because it is not there, but in the sense that it is not the reality of what is.

The other person you observe is not the reality. The reality is how that person subjectively feels. This is something you can never observe by looking outward. You can observe only their movements, and from that you form an opinion of the person and determine whether or not you like them. You cannot observe what's happening inside them.

If you sit in front of a group of people and watch them meditate, you cannot really know what's going on, even if you have the ability to see auras. Seeing people's auras is similar to studying a brain scan of the group. You may detect some changes in the activity of different centers of the brain, which may make you conclude that the individuals must be thinking in a certain way. You would not be able to be in touch with the climate, or atmosphere, within which those thoughts are taking place, as this cannot be seen.

Ashtavakra says observing what is outside is an illusion in the sense that it doesn't tell you anything about the reality of what is present. Exactly the same process is occurring when you look into a mirror. You may observe your face in the mirror, but that does not tell you anything about yourself. If you observe the inside – your climate and atmosphere – then the image in the mirror becomes meaningful.

THE ACT OF PROJECTION

Let's take an example. Say someone is insulting you, telling you off. Now you have a choice – either you can react to it, which means you react to the outside world (your observation that the person is telling you off), or you can begin to observe what is happening inside you.

Observing the person telling you something is meaningless. There is not the slightest possibility of progress or learning when you are reacting or just observing what is happening outside yourself. Instead, observe what happens inside yourself. Do not react, Ashtavakra says, to the outside movement. There is nothing to gain from observing it. The person who is offending you, for whatever reason, is not what you should observe. You don't know what that person is feeling. They may express their feelings, but do you know where they are coming from? You can know what's happening only if you direct your observation toward yourself, and in doing this, something dramatic occurs.

Ashtavakra returns constantly to this point when the mirroring and projecting stops. Projection is when you are constantly focused on observing others by wondering, "Do they like me?" or "What do they think of me?" Then you reflect back to yourself the information that you believe you have found. You begin to act accordingly, relative to how others seem to be reacting to you. This is a dreadful and destructive way of dealing with yourself and as Ashtavakra says, it puts you in bondage.

This is a problem all parents face. The emotional level of a young child is not well-structured, and psychology uses the ugly term *role model* in an attempt to explain what a child needs to learn from its parents. At the beginning of a child's life, he simply observes his parents, watching how they do or don't react to what he is doing. Therefore the child's first consciousness is not his own, but the parents' consciousness reflected back onto the child. If parents are not careful, they may at this stage create early neurosis in the child. The child must learn through the guidance of the parents.

If parents don't react to the child, he will be able to learn to reflect his own feelings, instead of projecting his parents' feelings back to himself. This way he will learn to observe properly. Otherwise the child becomes a little copy of the parents, and this will continue into later life.

The less you are able to learn the art of observation the more you will be a copy of your parents. For example, if you are born into a family bound by Christian values, you may be too afraid to ever step out of this role modelling because of what others may think. If your self-image and value comes out of what others think of you, this is the worst form of imprisonment that anyone can imagine.

THE ART OF OBSERVATION

The way out of this prison is to stop being influenced by the actions of others toward you. The first reaction is always to try to defend your position when someone acts toward you in a way that you don't like. Before you begin to defend yourself, ask the question. "What is happening inside of me," not "What does it mean?" A wise person stops the defense immediately, because the defense takes away energy available to observe what is actually happening within you.

Each time someone acts in a particular way toward you is an opportunity to practice the art of observation, if you just keep your attention on yourself. The moment you react, the possibility of choice and the space to see what is happening inside you are lost.

THE SPACE OF NO REACTION

This is profound wisdom offered by Ashtavakra. He states very clearly what observation really means: only in that process of constantly observing what is happening inside you is there the possibility of freedom. Only by not caring, not being dependent on outside influences, can you be free. In Time Therapy we call this the art of no reaction. There is no moral value attached to it, nor does it result from being too afraid to act. We cultivate this art because no reaction is the way to freedom.

Ashtavakra says, "Remember you are the one pure awareness." How can you have awareness if you always derive your value from the actions of other people toward you? And this refers to all actions, not just the negative ones. Sometimes it's easier to deal with negative actions than with positive actions. It is much more dangerous to fall into the trap here and end up in the same prison as a result of the adulation of others toward you. Then you suffer terrible loss when suddenly there is no more adulation, no more positive action coming toward you.

Celebrities can tell you, for example, about the deep depression they go through once their fame has ebbed.

How can you be yourself if you are relying on people liking you? At least when they are against you, this can be rationalized by saying that they don't understand you, or how stupid they are. You can then avoid them and escape from them. You can't escape the people who love you, admire you, and find you especially good. You cannot even avoid them, and it is then that the problems begin.

So even when people act positively toward you, Ashtavakra urges you to observe the inside. Your being and your value as a person cannot be derived from the actions of others – it has to be totally observed within yourself and only then can you have total awareness.

Your bondage is this – you see the others and not yourself as the observer. Bondage means a form of dependency. You observe if someone is reacting positively or negatively toward you and out of that you define yourself. This is split awareness. Ashtavakra calls it split brain, split mind. Awareness can be total only when there is no fear.

AWARENESS AND OBSERVATION

If you are dependent on observation of the outside, on how someone reacts toward you, there is always fear about whether they will continue to react positively or turn on you. Fear reduces awareness. It is in the nature of the mind not to want to see the whole picture.

This can be extremely helpful. For instance, when you are terminally ill and in a deep depression as a result of it, it is helpful to have the mind come in and ignore the fact that there may be a lot of fear about dying. Or imagine you have a handicapped child whom you know will never be the same as other children, and as she grows you see her suffering as a result of that limitation. The mind's ability to ignore some of this can make it easier to survive through a difficult situation.

The price for this ability to ignore the big picture, however, is partial awareness. Ashtavakra says complete awareness is necessary for enlightenment; therefore, to begin with, you have to radically break this bondage.

The bondage breaks when you stop the habit of observing the outside. It's not something you can practice. There is no technique. You simply have to stop observing the outside. Your eyes are open, your senses are there, you are aware of everything. See the distinction between awareness and observation. Being aware of everything is not observation. Observation is awareness together with reflection about the awareness. So, while you are aware of everything going on outside, the observation is occurring on the inside. There is no need for reaction toward the outside. Reactions will always show you that complete observation is not present.

No Separation

Ashtavakra strikes once more by saying, "I am an individually projected life." Drop this illusion, he says, and also the feeling of inner and outer. We have just understood that observation always has to be of the inside, but then he urges us to drop this idea or feeling of inner and outer, and awaken the thought that you are the unchanging conscious, the non-dual soul.

This is brilliant. This shows he was a master in observing the brain long before the discoveries of modern science. Each awareness and each observation can be perceived only through feelings; any thoughts occur afterwards. First there is a feeling and then you put it into a thought. Ashtavakra says observation must be so pure that it is an observation in the sense of awareness in reflection. This reflection does not include feeling and thought.

Hundreds of years later, Jesus used a similar expression when talking with his disciples. He asked them if they had thought about the answer to a question they had put to him, and then he urged them to *see* the answer.

Seeing, or observing, is neither thinking nor feeling. Ashtavakra says when it comes to awareness, the inner versus the outer no longer has a role to play. On the outside there are some feelings, on the inside there are some feelings. The usual state is one where on the outside someone has offended you, and you defend yourself. There is a feeling of anger outwardly, and on the inside a feeling of depression, of frustration and fear, another form of bondage.

Have you observed how often we deal with life this way? We feel a certain way toward the outside because we do not want to have problems, and the mind tells us that the outside world decides how we will feel about ourselves. On the inside, there is a feeling of being misunderstood, and so we are constantly bordering on a mild state of schizophrenia. What a bondage all of this is. We are split minds, as Ashtavakra puts it – on the outside one feeling, and on the inside, another feeling at the same time.

Ashtavakra tells us to stop all this. There is just oneness. The one unchanging, conscious, non-dual soul, and that unchanging, conscious, non-dual soul is not placed anywhere. That's what he means when he says, "You are the observer of all" and later, "There is all one, there is no you and me." Consciousness is consciousness. We are consciousness, not your consciousness or my consciousness.

So the division between inner and outer feeling is another form of bondage, part of a prison created by the mind. You are the oneness of consciousness – the one observer of all.

OBSERVING THE WHOLE

Now listen carefully, because Ashtavakra is very precise in his use of language. He doesn't say you are the one observer, he says you are the observer of all. How can you observe all if you are only a part? The part can never observe the all, the whole. Only the whole can observe the whole. So you are the one pure awareness, he says, which has burned the forest of ignorance. The bondage is the ignorance of split awareness of the inner and outer, the feelings and thoughts, the constant observation of the outside instead of just observing.

Whatever you observe, even on the outside, does not have any meaning if it is not at the same time connected with the inside, where the inside and the outside become one. If I cut out of your brain the emotional center, the language center, part of the limbic system of reflexes, you would be a zombie. You could watch as much as you like of the outside, but as you would be unable to observe yourself, there would be no meaning to any of it.

Have you observed that this is exactly what happens, in a less dramatic way, to a depressive person? When you are happy, or newly fallen in love, and you see a rose in a garden, you think, look at this rose, and what a beautiful day it is today! However when you are depressed, you will not see the rose or think the day is beautiful. The beautiful day will even become a problem. It is unpleasant to have a beautiful day when you are really depressed, simply because in depression there is no longer the ability to bring the inner and outer to oneness – you have a split mind.

THE FREEDOM OF ONE MIND

Ashtavakra says the split mind has to become the one mind. The one mind is beyond the split mind. It is still your mind because you still have a brain, but in the words of Krishnamurti, you now have an "intelligent" mind, which is no longer a split mind. And only then do you go beyond sorrow, says Ashtavakra.

How can there be no sorrow if you are not free? And let me repeat, freedom is not a blissful state of enlightenment. Freedom is there when you stop observing and reacting to the outside. This is the simple, easy step to freedom. It's everybody's choice whether to get to this freedom or not.

Let's be very clear here. Even if you are 100 percent right in a confrontation with someone, just observe the space inside yourself instead of reacting. This is what underpins the stories about how a Zen master may hit a disciple, and the disciple then gets enlightened.

Realization means the end of action toward what is coming at you, even if you are offended without justification. Just accept what's coming, observe what's happening inside, and you have freedom. Even in the most unjust situation, do not react.

In the first six years of my life I experienced tremendously unjust acts. When I was eleven years old I lived with a family for a whole year away from my adoptive parents. My room was in a cellar and after dinner at 6:30, as this family had two of their own children, they would send me down into the cellar so that they could have quality time with their own children.

Imagine what it was like to be eleven years old, to be down there in the cellar on my own each evening and every weekend for an entire year. It was like being in a prison.

The best thing to do in a situation like this is to get enlightened! There was no point in fighting against something in which there was no chance of winning, no point in complaining to the adoptive parents who didn't want to see or understand. The only way out was to see that freedom in this cellar was possible the moment I stopped reacting.

Not reacting does not mean becoming passive. It means just being totally in observation of whatever is there so you have the choice every second to observe what is actually happening inside. Whenever someone acts toward you, you immediately have the choice of observing the outside or moving into freedom by observing only the inside. This is not something you can learn or train for, or find a clever device or technique that will help. It's a question of making this choice every second of the day.

Ashtavakra exhorts you to realize that if you want to be free and out of bondage, you must stop the observation of the outside. What naturally follows is the ultimate bliss. Once you are free, not the slightest opinion of someone else can trouble you. You can now freely think about their opinion. How can you freely think about someone else's opinion when you are in reaction mode, and therefore not free?

THE POWER OF REBELLING

In a reactive state you can never really learn. Every opinion that you do not see in freedom creates a form of resistance. When someone is proud of you, you feel a little embarrassed; that's resistance. When they are against you, you get a little annoyed; this is also resistance. Only in freedom can you really learn from other people.

This is why children at a certain age have a need to rebel against their parents. This is because they need to find their own identity. Identity here means their space, within which only they decide who they are, and not someone else from the outside. For a certain amount of time they have the need to reject every opinion from the outside. Crises at this time are very often the first steps toward shaping their own personality. Do not interfere too much with them during this time.

Remember, Ashtavakra says that only when that bondage no longer exists is there freedom and ultimate bliss. Then there is freedom to really communicate with others, and in that moment, he says, the imaginary, illusionary world is no longer.

You all know of this imaginary world, the projection of an idea in your mind toward the outside. Ashtavakra explains that all this *maya* evaporates whenever observation is made toward the inside; then you begin to perceive reality as it is.

AS YOU THINK, SO YOU ARE

As you are only consciousness, being in your own conscious observation brings you to reality. This is what the word *enlightenment* really means – to awaken. To wake up to what? To the reality of pure consciousness. Knowing this, Ashtavakra tells us to wander through life happily. He who considers himself free is free, and he who considers himself bound is bound, because in this world the proverb is true, "As you think, so you are." Now this is brilliant, but do not misunderstand it by taking it superficially. As you think so you are. What does he mean?

The brain does not make the distinction between real happenings and imagination. Take the classical example of hypnosis. Hypnosis is a state where the split mind is less active. In scientific terms you would say the hypnotic mind is in one of the windows of the alpha wave state, i.e., a fore-trance state. If a hypnotist told you that you were now becoming very hot, you would become very hot.

The ability of the brain to do this arises out of evolution. When a lion attacks a gazelle, the gazelle does not feel fear or pain at the moment of attack. The brain just goes into a state of hypnosis. Nature would be incredibly brutal if this did not happen. So as a part of this evolutionary process of the brain, we still retain this capacity. That's why we use hypnosis or deep trance states to influence thinking. In another example, in your dream you see the lion chasing you as real, and you run. You may even wake up in a panic. Your imagination is sometimes even stronger than reality.

In modern terms, we would call this conditioning. To believe in a religion is conditioning. It has no truth to it. A truly religious person could never belong to a religion.

In your imagination, how you perceive God can be so powerful that it makes you afraid of God – what madness! You have no experience, in reality, of God, and yet you are afraid of your God. Similarly, you have never experienced hell – where, in the Christian religion, bad people go when they die – however, you are afraid of hell because you are conditioned into believing it exists. Another example of conditioning is nationality – we imagine ourselves to be Swiss or Greek or British, but this too is just an image we have of ourselves.

Conditioning is so pervasive that when we meet someone and over time get more familiar with them, we assume we know them. In fact, what we are doing is projecting the image we have about them. Then we may turn against them if the image we have of them doesn't fit with what's happening on the outside, in reality.

This is how conflicts arise. When the ideas we have do not conform to the outside, we do not stop and question these images. Instead, we usually hold on to our idea as being right and insist that the outside is wrong. For instance, I have the idea that there is a God, and then a stupid idiot like Ashtavakra comes along and asks, "Where is this God? Have you ever seen a God?' Remember that Ashtavakra asks us not to observe the outside. Praying to God is observing the outside.

REALITY AND PROJECTION

The brain has a tremendous ability not to be able to differentiate between reality and ideas. These ideas, these conditioned belief systems, are so strong when someone is against you that you will accept their image of you as confirmation of who you are. All this, because you are observing the outside. You then begin to turn against yourself, and the idea that you are not good enough becomes a reality. As you think, so you are.

Ashtavakra says this is so dangerous because you cannot have an idea without projecting it. To give life to an idea or a feeling you need to project it to the outside – to someone or something. If ideas were to just stay within your head, they would vanish. The image of God has no meaning if you don't project it, so you build temples, churches, or a cross to give it life. The idea "I am something" has to be projected, so we have to fulfill our imagination, otherwise it has no meaning. Suddenly we have the feeling no one is for us, that everyone is against us, simply because we have projected the idea to the outside.

You fulfill your own ideas and sometimes you do it because you want desperately to be right about that idea, otherwise you would have what is called a spiritual crisis. I am convinced that a lot of misery and psychological problems are based on trying desperately to bring the image we have of ourselves into action.

Let's take a very superficial example – superficial in the sense that I am oversimplifying it here. Repeatedly you are told you are not really worth anything. Let's say you are a girl. You are told you should behave in a certain way and your body should be like this or that. Over time, you develop an image of yourself that you are not beautiful, that you are not worthy of having a relationship, and that no one seems to want you.

Now that image will always dissipate whenever there are men present who act positively toward you. In order to defend the image of yourself, you will have to find a way to project it, to create your own bondage so that it really does work. When a man likes you, you may try to find a way to see what is not good in him. Doing this keeps your image of yourself alive.

Ashtavakra says this is dangerous, another part of the prison. "As you think, so you are" means not only that you have an inside image – that in itself wouldn't be a problem. For instance, you can think of an elephant, and that does not mean you now project that elephant and try to become an elephant or live with an elephant.

An image becomes dangerous when it is connected with feelings and emotions, because then it works or is kept alive through projection. In fact, Ashtavakra is saying this is precisely the problem with enlightenment. You have an inside image of what enlightenment means – something pure and perfect, without any weakness, and no one disliking anything about you. Everything you have ever said will be totally gone and you will be very intelligent.

This image can survive only if you project it to the outside, and as enlightenment is exactly the opposite of that, you end up feeling more stupid. You don't feel at all great or special, so you sit there trying hard to become enlightened, projecting that image of enlightenment. This image actually becomes the barrier to enlightenment.

THE SERPENT OF EGO

This is why Ashtavakra constantly insists that you must stop "doing." Using the image of a snake for the ego, he asks, you think you are the doer, so has the black serpent of ego bitten you? Whenever you think you must *do*, he says, you have been bitten by the snake of ego. By not being the doer, you drink the nectar of trust and can be happy.

Be aware that he is not saying stop doing. When you read Ashtavakra you have to read every word carefully and inquire as to what it means. He could say you are not the doer, and therefore drink the divine nectar and be happy, but no, he says drink this divine nectar of trust. Trust implies that you have no free will, which means you do not have the illusion that you can decide everything, because if you are enlightened, you cannot really make decisions about your life.

Let me give you two simple examples. Even if some people would like to believe differently, did you decide to be born? It's life's evolutionary process that you were born, whether you accept it or not. Are you going to decide when you die? Even if one commits suicide, they do not really decide freely and independently to die. And are you with your free will going to decide how your process of death will be? It will happen when it happens, whether you like it or not.

Now if your birth and death happen without your free will, why do we think that everything in between can be managed by us? Life does not need managers. Life needs creatures who live it. Therefore Ashtavakra says I am not the doer, drink that nectar of trust and be happy.

If you stop doing because you realize that not doing is a good strategy, and therefore you have a motivation for not doing, the motivation is once again the black serpent, the snake of ego. It's still about trying to achieve, it's still the black serpent biting you. So the question is, what is the connection between not doing and trust?

THOUGHT PROCESSES

First we have to look at thoughts. In the last five years, doing a little research on the brain together with other people at the university, I have come across something quite astonishing. Many people are trying to find out what is happening in the brain. They then publish their findings in a book. There are lots of ideas about what consciousness is, but have you ever read a book or scientific paper that explains the foundation of thoughts? This is ignored, simply because no one knows how thoughts come into being. Even the most down-to-earth scientist who believes that the brain is similar to a computer, i.e., just an electrochemical reaction, knows that the brain can create a thought like "I am."

This is a miracle. How can an electrochemical reaction create a thought? If this is how it is, then it is a miracle. Consequently, the scientists have a problem – how will they explain the miracle? No one knows, including myself, how this miracle occurs. A thought arises, I observe that, and it passes again. A chain of thoughts. I can break it into thought patterns, sentences, or words, because between each sentence, word, and letter there is a gap. This I can observe, but I cannot observe how the thought has come into being. I can observe it when it actually appears. I can be conscious of the presence of thoughts, but I cannot see how a thought is born. This is the miracle.

In Time Therapy we say thinking comes into being in two ways: the associative thought process (which is similar to the process Ashtavakra discusses) and the motivative thought process. In the associative thought process, whenever you think of something, it immediately connects with other thoughts you have, with images, pictures, and memory in what is an endless structure of association. This is because your brain is a holographic memory bank.

The associative thought process is in fact the process of memory. You think of an elephant, for example, and immediately you have an association with a memory, experience, or picture of an elephant. Without memory there would be no associative thought process. We say that the associative thought process is something you can only observe. You cannot get rid of it; otherwise, you would not have memory. A person with Alzheimer's, for example, has no memory.

The motivative thought process is directional – you start to think in a directed way about something, for example, you enquire, "What is God?" Now while the motivative process is occurring, part of the associative thought process comes into being, so we have the activation of what has been memorized along with the appearance of new, original thought. The associative thought process might be described as being like a brainstorming exercise.

The motivative thought process is directed toward finding something new while being aware, through the art of observation, of disconnecting from the associative thought process, which will always interpenetrate this process. This is the doer. This is the part you use to think about something and argue and find out something. This is brilliant if you want to construct a new car that produces no pollution. Then you have to think in new ways – this is beautiful, and good for the outside world. However it becomes destructive if you use it to change something about yourself.

This is why mystics like Buddha, Jesus, Mohammed, and Rumi make the distinction between the material and subtle levels. The motivative thought process has tremendous power but becomes a problem when used on yourself. You are not an object, not a motivation of materialism, says Ashtavakra. This is why he tells us to separate from the body consciousness.

The body is like a car. It's pleasant to drive in a car that functions well, however you have to understand that the car is not you. And the motivative thought process therefore must not be used on this level. Note what Jesus and others have all said: all your knowledge is not going to help. While it is good to have knowledge, just be aware that knowledge is part of materialism and not consciousness. Consciousness does not require knowledge. Consciousness does not need your history, and this presents a problem for psychology, which in fact is about your history. So the motivative thought process, if it is used for understanding yourself, turns into the form of doing.

THE PROCESS OF DOING

Now what's the process of doing? Every doing involves an action, otherwise it is not doing. Action comes out of impulses of thinking.

Even the tiniest of actions, for example, just moving your finger, occurs through an impulse of thought. That's why in science there is a distinction between the two nervous systems. There's the nervous system that works automatically, instinctively, and does not require thinking – according to Time Therapy, this is connected to the associative thought process. Instinct is the associative thought process.

At the other extreme we have intuition, which is the end of

doing, and in between the two is the action born out of the motivative thought process. So every doing demands an action. The action comes out of thought impulses. Therefore every doing originates with thinking, with the motivative thought process.

CREATING DESIRE

How does action, which first requires thinking before it can come into being, arise? In Time Therapy we say it arises through desire. Desire creates thought, so each doing that originates with thinking comes out of desire. Each desire, in turn, is first an emotion. For whatever reason, most of the time you are in a state in which there is no freedom. This is either because your observation is turned toward the outside, accepting what is coming toward you as a definition of who you are, or together with the internal image you have of yourself, projected outward. Consequently there is always a feeling of imbalance and a sense of not feeling content. That feeling creates desire, and only then the thought of exactly which desire it is arises. You first experience it as an energy of not feeling whole, feeling that something is missing. Now how can you feel bliss if you are not free?

As long as your observation is based on the outside, you are bound to create desire. It is impossible not to feel misery when you depend on all the opinions and reactions of others. Out of this are born all the desires imaginable.

WAKING UP

The desire to become enlightened shows that you are not free. Freedom does not create desire for enlightenment. So desire, the energy of misery, creates the thought of doing. Of course we could then say just be free. Freedom is there when you stop observing the outside, says Ashtavakra, and you have to make this choice every second. If it is this simple, why haven't we all already done it? It is so difficult to see this because it cannot be grasped intellectually.

Enlightenment is not a specific state. You wake up and you see that of course freedom is in observing the inside. That's enlightenment. Stop nurturing the image of what enlightenment is. It is simply an awakening to what freedom is, therefore, it is the ending of desire. So the question is, how does one stop desire if one cannot just be awakened? Let me repeat, desire arises when you are not free. Freedom cannot be present when you are observing the outside.

We are no longer concerned about how to observe the inside. We are asking how one can stop desire. You cannot start to observe inside and hope that desire will fall away, because if you start to observe the inside out of misery, you are still doing. You are activating the doing while observing the inside, which needs concentration. This becomes a trap.

Let me give you an example. If, as it's said, enlightenment is the end of the ego (the I) then the I cannot become enlightened. This is impossible. The I cannot reach enlightenment because enlightenment requires the ending of it.

To repeat: if the end of ego brings enlightenment, then obviously the ego cannot be enlightened. It's not that the ego doesn't exist in the state of enlightenment, it's that the ego just can't reach enlightenment – it is impossible. This is the only thing you really need to see to get awakened. You get enlightened simply because the ego drops away by itself.

In 1974 I suddenly realized that my whole body structure and everything in me had absolutely changed. I will never know whether it happened in one second or over a few hours. I have no conception of time in relation to it. All the feeling of heaviness of body and mind just dropped, not because I was doing something, but simply because there was absolutely nothing.

When the I is no more, there is enlightenment, but the I cannot execute it. Enlightenment is not about imagining that you are a perfect being – it is just the awareness that if enlightenment or freedom is the end of the split mind, then the split mind cannot be the tool with which to reach it.

How can we get to that point without the need for understanding or self-consciousness? Self-consciousness is part of the split mind, and the more the split mind tries to understand and to do, the less any awakening is possible. Ashtavakra gives hints by referring to outside observation versus inside observation, the illusion of the I versus the subjective feel.

He says stop the illusion that you are an individual that you project into this world through imagination. The only way I know – and I can go only from my own observation – is through the passive observation of desire.

As long as you are not free, there is misery even if you are materially comfortable, as all material possessions and object-orientation fails to fulfill. I am not suggesting that you become poor. We are talking about how everything, including knowledge, is materialism. Therefore as long as I am not free, despite all this that makes life easier, there is still desire. So I have to start to observe the desire passively, and that's why Time Therapy developed Modern Meditation.

OBSERVING DESIRE

So to summarize, to do something requires first an act of thinking. This is the motivative thought process. We know now that you don't get to freedom by acting. The doing, or the act of thinking about doing, arises out of desire. Therefore each desire builds up as energy until it's in consciousness. There is a gap between the impulse, the knowing of the desire, and the action. Between the desire and the action is space – scientifically shown to be half a second long. So passively observing desire simply means to observe the space between the arising desire and the action without getting into the action. Observe the desire, because that cannot be avoided as long as there is no freedom. You cannot command that there be no more desire – that would lead to a repression of desire. Don't get into action; just observe the desire, the space.

That's what I call the passive observation of the desire. Observe it for as long as you can until you suddenly wake up to the truth that enlightenment is the absence of the desire. Ashtavakra calls the absence of desire, bliss. Remember that Ashtavakra finished the second sutra by saying that you are the unchanging, conscious, non-dual soul.

THE THIRD SUTRA

Oh son, long have you been caught in the bondage of perceiving yourself as the body.

Cut this bondage with the sword of knowing I am awareness, and be happy.

You are alone, void of action, self-illuminated, and innocent.

Your bondage is this – that you practice samadhi.

You are permeating this universe. You are the thread within it.

You are pure consciousness by nature. Do not become small-minded.

You are without expectations, unchanging, self-sufficient, the abode of serenity, of boundless intelligence and unperturbed.

Hence have faith only in consciousness.

Know that which has form is false and know the formless as unchanging and everlasting.

From this true understanding, one is not born in the world again.

Just as a mirror exists in the image reflected in it and also exists apart from the reflection, God is within and outside this body.

Just as the one all-pervading sky is the same within and outside a pot, the eternal everlasting Brahman is the same in all.

ASHTAVAKRA RETURNS OVER AND OVER AGAIN TO HOW the bondage can be broken through observation. Cut this bondage with the sword of knowing. I am awareness. I am observation. And therefore be happy. His goal, if you can call it a goal, is so simple and so clear. Use the instrument of observation, but not to look toward the outside. Be awareness, not as a tool to separate you from the outside, creating duality, but as a tool of non-duality. Note that he says, I am awareness, not, I have an observation.

When you read Ashtavakra carefully you understand that the words *I am* mean that there is no distinction between the observer and the observed. One *is* that state of observation. The problem in understanding this lies in the struggle of the mind to become an observer. The mind can understand intellectually what it is to be the observer. It even understands that it should observe the inside and not the outside. But the mind is saying "I should," not *I am* the observer, who is also observing at the same time.

BEING THE OBSERVER

Why can't the mind "do" observation? This is because observation is our nature. You are observation. There is no distinction between you observing and you being observation. Take a very simple example. When you look at something, you are aware that you observe without doing the observation.

When you feel or sense something, you are aware that you feel or sense something without saying, now I feel, sense, think, or observe. The observation is you; therefore you can never escape observation. Observation is not a process of doing; it is a continuous product of living, of being.

You cannot avoid observation even if you are not cognitive, which in the mystical sense means being "in emptiness." Even if you were unconscious you could not stop observation. You do not stop observation even when asleep because you *are* observation. This is why you are able to dream. You wake up in the morning and you are not confused about what has happened. You know very well that you have slept, even if it has been a deep sleep, and this is because you are that observation – it cannot be avoided. In fact, one is nothing other than observation. The "I am" of Ashtavakra, in its real sense, is to always know that I am observation, because the observation happens without any effort. Even the most relaxed state – when you try to do absolutely nothing – is a contradiction, because trying to do nothing is in fact doing a lot. Even in a state of absolute relaxation, you may avoid thinking, or feeling any sensations, or you may be totally out of the body, but you cannot avoid observation, because you are observation. This is what Ashtavakra means by saying be aware, cut the bondage with the sword of knowing that I am awareness, and be happy.

Whenever Ashtavakra offers a deep insight, he always ends the sutra with "Walk happily" or "Be happy." He means that whenever you are that observation, whenever you are there fully present, there is no other state than happiness, bliss. Freedom is the ending of misery – desire – and therefore there must be, he says, "the movement of happiness." He says that once you have deeply, i.e., intuitively (not intellectually) understood that you are awareness and observation, you then suddenly realize you are alone.

THE END OF SEPARATION

The word *alone* simply means that there is no longer a separation between you and me. Alone is not about loneliness. Alone is about the ending of separation. This is misunderstood in so many spiritual communities where people isolate themselves and think they are enlightened because they are able to sit for twenty years alone on a mountain top.

On the spiritual level, *alone* means that there ceases to be a distinction between mine and yours. Of course, there is always a distinction on the physical level between your body and my body, but on an energy level there is oneness – alone is all one. In a group, if there is a group energy field, the oneness of me and of you melts into the one group. This is what is meant by alone.

Ashtavakra goes on to say that this state of being alone is void of action. This is because there is no longer a doer, an ego, I, me, or self.

In some Buddhist traditions, the phrase *void of action* is translated into *emptiness of action*. Ashtavakra (and I agree with him) does not believe in emptiness of action. Action here is never born out of self-interest, i.e., out of what is good for me. Action derives from what is good for the whole.

Void of action refers to the action of the wave becoming the ocean. The essence of the wave in the sea is not described by the shape of the wave; it is the water. Ashtavakra says the essence of a human being is not a form, i.e., not the body, not the split mind. The essence is consciousness. This is beautiful. Enjoy it if you experience a wave, i.e., form, but be aware that this is not your essence.

Jesus would have called *void of action* the ending of selfishness. I prefer Ashtavakra's void of action simply because the word selfishness translated into mind consciousness terms can be very destructive. Some people will call others selfish and themselves selfless, and this exact distinction between selfish and selflessness is part of creating ego.

The question is not whether someone is more selfish or less selfish. These are all ego games. The question is, do I realize that I am awareness? Can I observe the essence, the state of alone, the void of action? Can I be with the wave but never forget the awareness of the essence, which is the ocean. This is what Ashtavakra means by cutting the bondage.

BONDAGE AND INNOCENCE

Ashtavakra then goes further and talks of being "self-illuminated and innocent." This is one of the most difficult parts to understand. I prefer the word *innocence* to the word *humbleness*, which, like *selfishness* and *selflessness*, can become very tricky when navigating through life. Innocence is something you cannot be proud of, but you can be proud of humbleness, and once you are proud, you cease to be humble.

So Ashtavakra talks of innocence. When I read of innocence in the context of "You are alone," void of action, self-illuminated, and innocent, it reminds me of one of the most famous sayings of Rumi. It has been deleted from most of his standard textbooks because it was deemed to be disagreeable! Rumi said, "Sell your knowledge and buy confusion." And then he continues, "Knowledge is only an opinion. Confusion is intuition."

Listen to this: Sell your knowledge and buy confusion. In Time Therapy we call confusion *insecurity*. Knowledge, as we pointed out, is beautiful on a material level, but it will never help you see yourself. The word *self-knowledge* is utterly stupid. Knowledge is beautiful when concerned with very practical things.

The teaching of philosophy and psychology tends to create the illusion of knowing. Philosophy should not be taught at universities. Psychology should be taught only to a certain degree, because even if you have read all the scriptures and all the philosophies, it has nothing to do with knowledge in the sense that Ashtavakra or Rumi refers to. Sell the knowledge, says Rumi. Today he would probably advise you to run away from the universities. Go to the university to train to become a medical doctor, an economist, or a member of any other profession in which you need to have basic knowledge. Philosophy is about studying people's interpretations of what someone has said. Rumi would ask you to be a Socrates yourself, rather than to make a study of Socrates. When it comes to understanding yourself, the only worthwhile university is the observation of yourself – no guru, no institution, no book will do the job. At all times remember, I am awareness, void of action. You can study scriptures, you may listen to talks, but be very clear in making the distinction between the wave, which is form, and the essence, which is the water. Then there can be no problem.

Rumi, however, doesn't trust that the mind is capable of doing this, so he says sell your knowledge. Knowledge will create the bondage of history, of the past. In fact, he says when you are stuck in the prison of knowledge, you are stuck in the past. Socrates is the past. Your mind has a tremendous ability to be part of what's new. Your heart has the possibility to invent Socrates all over again. This way it's fresh and new. Rumi is asking you not to become a parrot, just a repetition of something. The only doorway to the new is confusion or innocence, he says.

Knowledge kills observation. Whenever you think you have the illusion of security, you stop observing. Your nature is observation, but you completely forget to use this in inner observation, because you think you know it all. When we think we know, we cease to listen to others. We just think we know. We listen out of politeness, but we don't really listen. Real listening is a total observation of yourself during the process of listening. All the rest is either being polite or trying to memorize.

During a talk, people often try to write down what the speaker is saying. This is nothing more than trying to accumulate knowledge. Rumi, if he were here today, would probably throw these people out. He says, "Buy confusion." This is the same as Ashtavakra's call to "be innocent."

CONFUSION CREATES OBSERVATION

The idea that you should know who you are is bound to create misery, as the I is constantly changing. There are about five different "I's" within each of us. The social "I" dictates how you behave in society, the private "I" dictates how you behave when you are alone, the relationship "I" determines how you behave with people you know well, the university "I" describes how you behave when you are at the university, the professional "I," when you are working.

If you are, as Ashtavakra always points out, only consciousness and if consciousness is something that cannot be described, then whenever you try to know who you are, you become more miserable. If we observe closely, we see that the I cannot be known, because it's a constantly changing phenomenon. It's like a monkey jumping from one tree to another.

Ashtavakra and Rumi claim that knowledge creates bondage, while confusion, which is the ending of knowing, creates observation. The beauty of a child is its innocence. What does the innocence of a child look like? It can be described as liveliness in total awareness. So Rumi says have the courage to sell your knowledge. There is nothing wrong with confusion and innocence, or insecurity. Security is a fine prison. You may have and need security on a material level, but this is not freedom. It is impossible, says Rumi, to find freedom through knowledge. Adhering to the known also makes it impossible to create anything new. This is what Ashtavakra meant by "self-illuminated and innocent."

THE BONDAGE OF MOTIVATION

Ashtavakra penetrates further by saying, "Your bondage is this – that you practice samadhi." The meditation teachers must panic when they hear this.

In a later sutra, he argues that meditation and the practice of meditation is one of the most useless forms you can engage in. Ashtavakra is not the only one to feel this way about the practice of meditation.

Much later, the Christian mystic St. John of the Cross said the first step in meeting God is to stop prayer and meditation, or contemplation, as he called it. Contemplation, he said, is the cultivation of images, and thinking that because you have these images, you are different from everyone else. But these images are the barrier to God.

Ashtavakra says your first bondage is in not observing, and the next bondage is that you practice samadhi. This has to penetrate deeply into your heart. In Time Therapy we say that as long as you meditate with the motivation to reach something, you are not meditating, and as long as you meditate being aware that you meditate, this is also not meditation.

The deep consequence of seeing this is that it seems to destroy a huge part of Buddhism – the practice of Vipassana or Zazen, for example – and it leaves confusion, innocence. There is, however, a very dangerous trap here that most people fall into.

The materialists, the capitalists, the doers, and the competitors could misuse this by saying "Stop all this nonsense of practicing meditation; the bondage is that you practice samadhi." But they miss the point. When Ashtavakra says "The bondage is that you practice samadhi," this has to be seen in the context of the bigger picture, i.e., that you are consciousness.

Ashtavakra advises only that the *motivation* for practicing must not be there. What's the motivation – is it desire? Be in meditation as often as you can, but don't practice meditation. That's the message. He does not say do not have any attitude or state of meditation. But if motivation is present, then there is a state of bondage. So one has to be careful not to take this advice out of context.

Ashtavakra says enlightenment is without "me" and therefore the "me" cannot get enlightened. Samadhi is a state that happens without the need for me to do anything, so therefore I cannot practice samadhi. The word meditation, in its process, is the end of doing anything. Meditation therefore is not a doer practicing meditation.

Here Ashtavakra goes to the root of waking up. Krishnamurti is another modern teacher who said this and who also was often misunderstood. He said meditation had to have no technique, no practice. What he meant was that the one that tries to do something cannot do what can be done only without anyone being present.

NOTHING TO DO

The best form of meditation sometimes happens when you sit in a train with absolutely nothing to do. You just sit there but you don't think consciously of meditating, and in doing so you slip into a state of meditation.

It's the same with observation. You cannot avoid observation, because it's your very nature. Also, you cannot avoid that state in which the split mind is no longer, because it is your nature. Therefore meditation does not need to be a practice. Just be there and wait to fall into it. Once you really start to be in touch with the inside an emptiness comes upon you. Meditation then happens by itself.

Ashtavakra is asking you not to practice samadhi because, just as with enlightenment, if your motivation is to achieve some goal, then you have created bondage. This happens because you are already pure consciousness by nature. How can pure consciousness attain samadhi through meditation, when it is already samadhi?

You search for yourself and never find yourself, because the self is always there. You are pure consciousness by nature, Ashtavakra says. In Time Therapy we would call this trying to find your "qualities." You don't need to reach or search for your qualities. You don't need to get rid of anything in order to get to your qualities.

The qualities, or the quality aura, are your nature. The energy body is your essence. The body, the mind, is just a wave – beautiful. But the wave without the ocean, the essence, is nothing.

Osho called form without essence artificial. It's as if you see a beautiful wave, but when you step into it you find that it's made of soft paper. Osho also asks you not to be artificial; be alive. Ashtavakra would say you cannot be alive through knowledge, you need innocence or Rumi's confusion or Time Therapy's insecurity. Pure consciousness is your nature. Then Ashtavakra says, as samadhi is without a doer, "Hence, therefore have faith."

FAITH AND BELIEF

Now why does Ashtavakra not use the word *belief*? Have you observed the tiny difference between belief and faith? In religion, it is said that having faith is a response to that which cannot be expressed, however in all the interpretation of this we are told that we must believe.

Ashtavakra makes an enemy of belief. Belief goes hand in hand with knowledge. He says faith always includes doubt. Spirituality confers absolutely no sense of authority even if some of the esotericists would love to have it otherwise.

You cannot believe in anything. Faith is the movement of trying to observe yourself with all the doubt you may have. Belief creates an image, image creates action, and action creates racism and fascism. Faith, however, leaves everything open.

Belief creates the idea that you can convince other people of something. Faith is something you can have only for yourself. It can never be forced upon other people. If you have faith in God, it would not matter that a philosopher tells you God does not exist. For you, God is there, but in your faith there is always a degree of doubt. Hence you will always see it, reach out to it, observe it anew.

Once you begin to *believe* in God your observations are dead. This is the problem with parts of modern Islam or the Christian church. Belief here creates different interpretations, therefore different actions of resistance. Faith is personal. Belief is social. Ashtavakra warns you not to have belief. Have faith instead and have it only for yourself. Never try to convince anyone else of it. In fact if you have faith, you will never try to convince anyone of it. However if you believe in something, you will get angry if others remain unconvinced by you.

Out of beliefs in various Gods, wars have been fought. The beauty of what was taught by the Buddha and by Ashtavakra is that they never came up with a concept of God or prophets. The Buddha never answered the question, is there a God? This is faith. He knows for himself alone because he has observed.

FAITH IN CONSCIOUSNESS

Look at the difference here. Knowledge is the ending of observation. Observation is the continuous observing of the new, the observation that there is something you may call God or consciousness, but it is not structured into a belief system. This is why the Buddha has never waged wars. A real Buddhist doesn't fight for Buddhism – if he does he has started a belief system and he is no longer a true Buddhist.

So have faith only in consciousness. You cannot believe in consciousness, because you could not know how to structure that. There is no object you can make out of consciousness. You are consciousness, Ashtavakra says in the first sutra, but then he says that you cannot be 100 percent sure of this. You cannot have a belief system, or an opinion about it, therefore you can only have faith in consciousness.

FORM AND STILLNESS

Ashtavakra then strikes again by saying, "That which has form is false and that which is formless is changeless and everlasting." This concept of form and formlessness comes up in all religions, but more so in Buddhism and Hinduism than in Christianity.

What exactly does the word *formless* mean if we place it in the context of Ashtavakra's sutras? Obviously, we can't claim that the body is formless.

A good illustration of this enigma is given in the story of the Zen master asking the disciple what he has understood after ten years of Zen practice. And the disciple says "that everything is an illusion." The Zen master hits him and the disciple says "ouch." The Zen master then asks him why he says "ouch" if everything is an illusion. This concept of the formless creates room for misunderstanding and leads to unreasonable suggestions – for example, that everything is an illusion.

Ashtavakra means something very precise when he talks of the formless being unchangeable and everlasting. What is unchangeable and everlasting? In the process of your observation, consciousness is changing, so that cannot be the everlasting or unchangeable.

But if you observe very carefully through the process of detaching yourself – as Ashtavakra says in the first sutra, by separating from the body – stillness is created. When you are deeply asleep there is also no form, no awareness of your body, and in that there is stillness. He says when there is faith, when you have stopped the bondage of practicing samadhi or enlightenment, when you see that you are pure consciousness in nature, then there is formlessness or stillness.

So what, then, is stillness? In Time Therapy stillness is defined as the absence of fear, but now we ask this question and try to see it anew, so as to get to another level of understanding. What is stillness? In the context in which Ashtavakra uses it, we see that stillness occurs when you stay with whatever is there without any desire to change it. Whenever you observe desire without action – action being the impulse – there is an awareness of space, and then there is stillness.

In other words, stillness is about having no resistance to the experience of the moment. There is a tremendous difference between the idea of freedom, which Ashtavakra uses so often, and the Buddha's peace. Both of these are connected with the phrase *void of action*. The difference between freedom and peace is like the difference between sea water and lake water. Both refer to the essence, but something different is implied by each. Freedom takes you way beyond peace. In total freedom there is not a trace of any peaceful feeling. Stillness brings peace.

If you can stay with what is there – the Buddha's *tathata*, or *suchness* – without a trace of desire to change it, what can the mind do? If there is absolutely no action for desire, the mind becomes tremendously passive. It falls into stillness. That's what all the mystics mean when they speak about being in the now. When there is absolutely no resistance against any experience that is happening in the moment, what can the mind do?

It has no energy for action. Action requires energy. Never forget that action cannot arise without the energy of thought or desire. If these aren't present, then the mind just falls into stillness. It becomes tremendously peaceful.

STILLNESS OF THE HEART

In the teachings of the Buddha or the *Bhagavad Gita* we can find reference to the stillness of the heart. What does this mean? Staying on the level of body consciousness, let's suppose you are in a situation where you can go absolutely nowhere. I return to my example of sitting in the damp cellar as an eleven-year-old boy. I could not go upstairs or outside of the house because I was too young to be out on my own in the evening. There was no radio or TV for distraction. I was not even allowed a book because they felt I needed to sleep.

When there is absolutely no way of changing a situation and you do not react against it, the whole system just falls into peace. Modern science has observed this behavior in animals; it is called the dead reflex. When this is accompanied by observation, then it is not paralysis, but passivity, which brings stillness.

The mind can be active only for as long as you feed it. The mind is not the enemy. Our mind has no objection to being still. It's the feeding of it that keeps the mind working. Just as a paper shredder will keep working as long as you feed it paper, the mind will do something with whatever you give it. Stillness is not a contradiction for the mind.

Ashtavakra says that once you have seen the formless and realize that the object, the manifestation, is not that which is really you; once you have seen that you are awareness and that you don't need to do anything; once you have seen that there is no need for samadhi because you are samadhi; once you have seen that the I cannot get enlightened because enlightenment is the absence of the I – then the whole mind falls into stillness.

Being with What Is

The Christian mystics tried to describe this state by talking of patience, of just sitting and waiting. This is a hundred times more difficult today than it was two thousand years ago. Our mind is like a hamster running in a wheel. It is much more difficult nowadays to avoid nourishing the mind. However, whenever you stay totally with what is, without any trace of desire, stillness is bound to happen. The desire to be enlightened stops you from staying with what is, because at the beginning of this process, *what is* is not the state of enlightenment.

So you find yourself split in two – one part trying to get enlightened and the other observing whether you've become enlightened – and therefore there is never stillness.

Stop the resistance against any experience, which is there from moment to moment, otherwise there can be no peace. This is precisely what happens when one dies. The suffering in dying goes on until you stop having resistance toward the experience. Once the resistance goes, there is tremendous peace and stillness, and this peace affects everyone present. Your mind doesn't affect anyone else very much, but your stillness – the falling into peace – has a profound effect on everyone. It is a powerful energy.

In my view, love is born out of stillness. It can never be born out of anything else. Have you observed that when you really love someone your whole awareness becomes tuned to listening to what the other person wants? This can happen only by observing the inside, and that's where the stillness comes from. Suddenly you stop doing and become a receiver. This is the paradox, and out of that receiving comes love. The act of giving is not love. When you become receptive, that is what creates love, because in that receptiveness you stop doing. Therefore the mind falls into stillness, the formless.

REFLECTING CONSCIOUSNESS

And then Ashtavakra takes us one step further. He uses certain words repeatedly, especially in the third sutra. Let's first look at the word *mirror*. He says in that stillness you become a mirror. The formless is a mirror. He first tries to explain this by saying that a mirror just reflects whatever is there, but when there is no longer any reflection, the mirror still exists.

This means that a mirror exists even when there is no longer any projection. It is always there. It reflects only what is there. God is a mirror. The one mind is a mirror. In fact, if Ashtavakra is correct with his observation that we are consciousness, we are then nothing other than carriers of lights, or mirrors. We reflect consciousness – that's the whole secret.

The universe is a mirror. That's what Martin Buber meant when he so beautifully said, "I can do nothing without God, but what would God do without me?" He is describing himself and God as mirrors. By saying that consciousness exists in the image reflected in it and also when there is no reflection, Ashtavakra is drawing a comparison between outside and inside observation.

What a revelation to see that one is nothing else than a carrier of light. To be a carrier of light you need light to reflect, to be a mirror. A mirror needs light so that you can see what is reflected in it. We are mirrors and light. The universe is endless, formless stillness and it comes alive through the reflection of our consciousness because we are this mirror.

So, remember that the two main bondages are first how you observe, and second the deep understanding that there is nothing for you to do. The doer cannot get enlightened, as enlightenment is the absence of the doer. And then, Ashtavakra says, once you have cut the two main bondages, you see that you are a mirror.

At the end of the sutra he says that with this understanding, one is not born in the world again. You see that he does not bother with reincarnation. He is not saying that when you reach enlightenment, you will not be born again. He says very clearly that through this true understanding, one is not born in the world again. The world refers to the nurturing of desires, the manifestation, the split mind.

THE STILLNESS OF EMPTINESS

What does Ashtavakra really mean by "true understanding"? He does not say "from this understanding," he says, "from this *true* understanding." Here he does not mean to claim that this is the truth, for if he had, he would have created a belief system, and we know that he did not have any time for beliefs. He has faith in faith.

Ashtavakra is saying that there is an awakening to the nature of being. He is saying that once you cut the ties of bondage, you wake up to the stillness of emptiness. The stillness of emptiness cannot be explained conceptually – it is up to you to find this in yourself. The awakening brings you into a state of stillness, of emptiness. I know only that out of this stillness of emptiness, the movement of love follows.

The nature of the stillness of emptiness cannot be

described. You must be the carrier of light, the mirror of reflection, which reflects the mind having come to stillness. The formless is our nature, and in moving with this formless-ness, like a leaf being carried by a breeze, you come to the stillness of emptiness.

THE FOURTH SUTRA

Stillness.

All things arise, suffer, change, and pass away.

This is their nature.

When you know this, nothing perturbs you, nothing hurts you, you become still.

It is easy.

Sooner or later fortune or misfortune may befall you.

When you know this, you desire nothing, you grieve for nothing.

Subduing the senses, you are happy; whatever you do brings joy or sorrow, life or death.

When you know this, you may act freely, without attachment.

What is there to accomplish?

All sorrow comes from fear, from nothing else.

When you know this, you become free of it, and desire melts away.

You become happy and still; the world with all its wonders is nothing.

When you know this, desire melts away, for you are awareness itself.

When you know in your heart that there is nothing, you are still.

SO FAR IN THESE SUTRAS, ASHTAVAKRA, LIKE THE BUDDHA and all the others after him, has pointed out that freedom, peace, and enlightenment cannot be attained through the efforts of the ego. The ego is in fact the barrier to enlightenment.

The picture we have of enlightenment as the way to freedom, peace, and compassion involves the ending of the ego. If this is true, Ashtavakra says, then the ego cannot be the instrument used to reach enlightenment. Clearly, then, the ego cannot experience enlightenment. Put simply, this means enlightenment occurs when experiencing stops, or the person that experiences is no more.

Now the mind simply cannot grasp this, nor can it see the point of becoming enlightened without being aware of the process. The mind wants to be able to know what is going on, and to be able to show off about it afterwards. This is because, truthfully, the mind doesn't aspire to enlightenment for the sake of bringing more peace into the world. It aspires to enlightenment because it wants to be better than others.

THE SPIRITUAL EGO

In order to see if it's improving, the mind needs experience. The motivation for enlightenment is to achieve a state that has been described by others, so that the mind can feel it has achieved something better than to be violent, naïve, or stupid. It can then claim to have become a religious entity. It cannot recognize the point in anything if it cannot describe what it has achieved. I call this the debate of a spiritual ego. The ego is dealing with the spiritual rather than the material, but it remains the ego nonetheless.

The mind can feel spiritual. If it is at a naïve stage of spiritual ego expression, it sees angels, talks about spirit guides and astral beings, and describes great wise men and women who come to help. But this is still ego.

The mind will argue that it needs to see whether its effort to be as good as possible is paying off. The mind believes that there is no point in trying to improve if it has no confirmation that it is becoming better. It needs to be able to compare. The ego is structured out of comparison. Children begin to develop an ego at about two to three years of age because then they are able to compare themselves to others. Without comparisons, things get very boring for the mind because you stop experiencing.

So the ego that desires enlightenment is 99.99 percent spiritual. It has a desire to become better, to become different, to change. But this motivation is the root of the I. Therefore enlightenment cannot happen while this desire exists. Only when there is the absence of any motivation can there be enlightenment.

Modern psychology and all the mystics encourage us to relax and forget about becoming better as there is nothing to achieve or change. But the mind mistrusts all of this, always believing it has to achieve something. So the question then is, if we cannot attain enlightenment through the I, how then do we do it? It's too simple just to say, well, do nothing. Rarely can the mind, even for a hundredth of a second, forget itself, and have a glimpse of samadhi. All the advice to relax and not worry about a thing sounds good, but is useless as a strategy to help the mind.

Of course we know that if enlightenment is the absence of the ego, then the ego cannot possibly reach enlightenment. We understand this. However, the part of us that is really longing for freedom wants to be sure that it reaches this freedom, even when the motivation is born 100 percent out of compassion. For example, Evelyn Underhill spoke of "the fire burning inside" to describe this need to know whether she had succeeded.

This part cannot be destroyed. That's why George Harrison sings in one of his songs about "sneaking around the corner" to bypass the ego. So we, too, have to go around the corner. Don't wage a frontal assault on the ego, as you will lose. But how do you bypass the ego? Whenever you fight directly with the I, you increase the I. Fighting always leads to the creation of more energy in a negative sense.

BYPASSING THE EGO

In this sutra, Ashtavakra describes something tremendously important. With this one sutra he goes to the root of the problem. He says very simply that all sorrow comes from fear and from nothing else. Here he underlines the fact that it is *fear* and *fear alone* that is at the root of sorrow.

In knowing this, he continues, you become free of fear, and desire melts away. This is because desire is born out of fear. Desire is the need to escape fear, to end fear. I want to be better or to understand because maybe then I will no longer have fear.

So Ashtavakra says the basic concern of human beings in proceeding toward liberation is how we deal with fear and with feelings. Perhaps this is why the old scriptures like the *Bhagavad Gita* advocate an end to thinking.

But how does a thought come into being? In Time Therapy we say that 80 percent of thoughts are motivated by fear. We would not need to think about the past if there was no fear. The thought "I'm afraid that so and so does not love me," triggers a chain reaction of thoughts such as "Why am I not better?" "What should I change about myself?" and so on. Have you observed that every so-called psychological understanding is based on explanations about the past?

Feelings trigger thoughts. A number of different forms of meditation have missed the point by focusing on the observation of thoughts. All sorrow comes from fear. Notice how the ego, which is structured in the past, is projected into the future. Thinking is a constant movement of the past projected into the future.

Classical paranoia is where this projection is taken too far. In paranoia, the past of the ego is projected fully into the future, so there is not a second of living in the now. This can happen only when there is a huge amount of underlying fear.

BECOMING STILL

Ashtavakra says that desire melts away when you grasp the fact that all sorrow comes from fear. You can also substitute the word *thinking* for *sorrow*, as 80 percent of our thinking is born out of fear. He says that in grasping this fact, you become happy and still.

Ashtavakra is very precise in his use of words. He doesn't say, you become happy. If he did, then the mind would step in and develop a concept about happiness. Here, Ashtavakra precisely describes happiness. You become happy and still.

Note that it's not about moving from fear to happiness. That would mean trying to find out how to reach happiness. This would increase the energy of the spiritual ego. No, he says, once you understand this, you become happy and still. Happiness that is born of stillness cannot be experienced as happiness, as such. Look at the depth of this wisdom.

In another sutra he talks about the realization that can arise through this stillness. He says, "I am not the body, nor is the body mine. I am awareness itself." When you know this, he says, you have no thought of what you have done or left undone. In this state of happiness with stillness, thought is not present. You become one, perfect, and unable to be split in two.

Stillness, as an energy process, can be described as the ending of description, explanations, and justifications. The ego derives energy through comparison. Comparing is the thought process of describing, explaining, justifying. Nothing needs to be justified if you do not have duality. Nothing need be explained if there isn't the split between the now and the past. Explanations and analysis require division into parts.

So Ashtavakra is in fact saying that we have to understand feelings. Because feelings give rise to thoughts, they are the energy drive for thoughts. So what are feelings? Just to say they are energy is not sufficient.

THE STRUCTURE OF FEELINGS

Based on Ashtavakra's sutra, we can now say that all sorrow is based on feelings. All sorrow comes from fear, but he insists that fear has something to do with feeling. This is why he starts the sutra by saying that all things arise, suffer, change, and pass away; this is the nature of form. But he also says that sooner or later fortune or misfortune may befall you. Happiness without stillness, joy without stillness, or bliss without stillness is as separating as fear.

This is why in Time Therapy we distinguish between two feeling states: fast feelings and slow feelings. Fast feelings stem from aggression and fear. Of course aggression has hundreds of different expressions, for example, greed or jealousy. But the foundation is simply aggression. To go further in the chain of feelings, aggression is always a symptom of fear. Here we are in agreement with Ashtavakra, who says all sorrow comes from fear.

Every one of us is familiar with fast feelings. They are called fast feelings because they trigger body responses that last for no more than three minutes. A body could not bear more than three minutes of pure aggression. After this acute phase, you acquire a chronic state of aggression. This chronic state of aggression vacillates between fear and an expression of some form of aggression, and then back to fear.

A number of body problems result from this vacillation

between aggression and fear. The body reaction to fast feelings ends after approximately three minutes, and then fast feelings are maintained by thought alone. The idea of the feeling takes over, although the feeling *per se* has ended.

The aggression is then no longer felt on the level of the body. It has become an idea, a complexity of thoughts. Aggression, *per se*, doesn't turn into a psychosomatic illness, as it is only three minutes long. It does disturb the body system when aggression becomes internalized as a thought. The chronic state always involves a thought structure.

This is why Ashtavakra says that once you see fear as the basis of sorrow, then you move to a state of no more thought. Feelings are not the problem. This is why you can use feelings to sail around the ego. It's when the feeling has become crystallized as an idea or a thought that it becomes a problem.

Christianity's entreaty to forgive is in fact asking you to stop nurturing negative thoughts toward someone. Negative thoughts will poison your own system. Feelings never poison your system, except when translated into thoughts. According to Time Therapy the way to get out of this thought trap of aggression and fear is to see that fear is a symptom of sadness. In doing so you move to what Time Therapy refers to as slow feelings. Sadness is a part of slow feelings, as are love, compassion, and bliss.

Slow feelings are less body-oriented than fast feelings, and are not quite so structured in a cause and effect relationship. They can be present for a period of time, but they are not sustained by thought. They are either there or they are not.

A THIRD STATE

Ashtavakra says something deeper. He doesn't even bother about fast feelings and slow feelings. He says once you see that all sorrow comes from fear and from nothing else, you become happy and still. To me, this means Ashtavakra is talking about a third state.

In Time Therapy we say that fast and slow feelings are born out of what we call the climate or atmosphere. Each one of us has a specific feeling climate. How, and to what extent, we express fast or slow feelings in daily life depends on this climate.

Modern psychology has made a huge mistake in confining its interest to feelings and thoughts, and attempting to show how different parts of the brain represent different feeling levels. Positive Psychology, developed in the US by Martin Seligman, has researched through studying PET scans why some people react to the same situation happily without stress, while others react in a traumatized manner. For example, someone who has been in a concentration camp can exhibit more calmness and peacefulness in comparison to someone who has had the best of everything in life.

This fundamentally misses the third level that Ashtavakra alludes to and it disregards that each person has a particular climate that will eventually dictate how they react. In Time Therapy, we say that this climate may be responsible for how you behave in life, i.e., what you feel on the first two levels, the fast and slow feelings, and how you think.

We are constantly active, and all this action results in consequences. The idea of karma arises out of this. Ashtavakra goes on to say that "whatever you do brings joy or sorrow, life or death. When you know this you may act freely, without attachment." He does not say when you know this, you act freely. He says you *may* act freely. In Time Therapy we say that whether you may or may not depends on your personal climate. It does not depend on your feelings of aggression or fear, nor on the love or happiness you feel in the moment.

Ashtavakra says you may act freely, without attachment. He asks, "For what is there to accomplish?" Fear is the process of comparing. Either you are better than the other and therefore you're afraid to lose this position, or you are not as good, and afraid that you may not improve. Is there anything to accomplish? He says of course there is not. This is why he says all sorrow comes from fear.

LOST CONNECTIONS

Once you have connected with the source, which means the climate, attachment falls apart. Let's take two classic examples from the field of psychiatry. When one works with people suffering from major depression, one frequently hears them say that they do not know who they are. They may express this by saying that there is no meaning in life, which translates into I don't know who I am, how I feel, or what is the meaning of "me."

A depressive person has totally lost the connection to their climate. They are on a roller coaster of self-pity, sadness, fear, or anger. They have lost the connection to their source, and therefore they need to be assisted in reconnecting. Sometimes this occurs through medication. Whatever means you use is perfect if it brings them back to the source – not to an I structure or a spiritual ego, but to the source, to that which is beyond the I.

There are different types of schizophrenia, but the most common shows itself as the strongest manifestation of fear possible. Fear is the signal that the connection to the climate is lost. In fact, one could say that the depressive person also primarily has a structure of fear; however, the fear is not personalized. In the schizophrenic person the fear is personalized, and beyond this is the loss of connection to the climate, the source.

In Time Therapy, we point out the paradox of this situation. You are totally dependent on other things, people, or situations, and on your fast and slow feelings, when you do not have a connection to the climate. However, you cannot get to the level of enlightenment if you are not structured in the climate. So what is this climate?

BEYOND THE EGO

Let's look again at the sutra. Ashtavakra says all sorrow comes from fear and from nothing else. When you become aware of this, you become free of it and desire melts away; you become happy and still.

The climate is beyond the ego. Happiness that is built on the ego – even if it is an advanced, spiritual ego – is still ego. Happiness that involves stillness is the absence of ego. Here, happiness is independent of outside influences, situations, or other people and how they react toward you. It is also independent of your thoughts, i.e., your concern about whether or not you have achieved.

The climate is a feeling born out of stillness. That climate can be polluted by thoughts and fast feelings. It is also possible that slow feelings may get in the way of connecting to the climate, so fast feelings – aggression and fear – are based far less on your history than on the absence of connection to the climate.

This climate, and the absence of fast or slow feelings, is very apparent in young babies up to about four months old. They just radiate a climate, an atmosphere. As they grow, they develop a consciousness about themselves. For instance, a wave of jealousy may develop out of the child's climate, and if the parents react to this, the child will become identified with it, and over time, the wave becomes a form. The child comes to believe that the wave (its jealousy) is more important than the ocean (its climate).

In this way, the mind begins to believe that thinking and feeling are more important than the climate. You cease to see the wood for the trees, and so you run, you fight, you try desperately to understand aggression and fear. Whenever you attach to thoughts, which are created by feelings, you lose the connection to the climate. You pollute the climate.

Ashtavakra says the world with all its wonders is nothing. He does not even want you to cling to the form of God, a form of beauty, a miracle. Enlightenment, he would probably say, is a joke. He says the world with all its wonders is nothing. And when you know this, then desire melts away, for you are awareness itself.

KNOWING THERE IS NOTHING

What does Ashtavakra mean when he says, "when you know in your heart that there is nothing?"

To know "in your heart" does not involve your thinking patterns and has nothing to do with feelings as we know them. Fast feelings are experienced in the solar plexus, and Ashtavakra isn't referring to this.

When he talks about *heart*, Ashtavakra is referring to your climate, your atmosphere. When you know in your heart that there is nothing, no wonder that then you are still. By stillness he means there is no longer a trace of even slow feelings. All you have now is only the third part of the feeling structure, which is the atmosphere. The only way to sneak around the spiritual ego, or any level of ego, is through stillness. Stillness is there when you know with your heart that there is nothing.

The chain of feelings is that aggression is a symptom of fear, and fear is a symptom of sadness. However when you also know that the expression of each aggression, each fear, each sadness, each love, each happiness is based on the climate, then there is no longer any desire to change anything. There is just stillness.

When aggression arises from out of the climate, the aggression dies away in a hundredth of a second. When love is born out of the climate – remember, we are talking of love as happiness and stillness – then this love will also transform into something different.

A holy person is not someone who is rid of feelings. However, these feelings, whether they are fast or slow, are totally based on the third force of feeling, which is the climate. This third feeling structure decides how you will live in your life, how you express yourself in this life. Of course you can pollute your climate with fast feelings or slow feelings and with thoughts, but this pollution can be cleared away. You have the possibility to re-establish the original balance. Ashtavakra says that this can happen through stillness.

How do you stop polluting your climate or clear away the pollution that exists? What is the way to stillness? Ashtavakra says all things arise, suffer, change, and pass away. As George Harrison sang, "All things must pass." Sooner or later, says Ashtavakra, fortune or misfortune may befall you, and when you know this, you desire nothing. You grieve for nothing. He then says something tremendously important. He says, "Subduing the senses, you are happy." Subduing the senses is a description of what happens when you fall into stillness. So how do you get to stillness?

Have you ever thought about what would happen if you could not project your ego into the future? In Time Therapy we say that 80 percent of our actions are not motivated by the past, but by the fear of what is going to happen in the future. If that fear were increased a little because of events in the past, this increase would be statistically insignificant.

This is what modern biomedicine means by stating that whatever is happening in the brain cannot just be explained by what has happened in the past. Eighty percent of our actions are based on the fear of what's going to happen in the future, meaning that we ask ourselves questions like, "Will I be loved? Will I be able to achieve? What will my future be like?" All sorrow comes from fear, says Ashtavakra.

So what would happen if one didn't project? You can project only your past. You cannot project what is now, you can project only your experiences, which you have compared, evaluated as good or bad, and then projected into the future. The energy of projection is fear. You can project only into the future through the energy of fear. What would happen if that were to stop?

SNEAKING AROUND THE EGO

In times gone by, the mystics would have said that once you stop projecting, you are in the now. But the now is a difficult concept. In Time Therapy we say that once you stop projecting, you are connected with the climate.

This atmosphere is something you cannot personalize. This is why Ashtavakra says that once you are so connected, you grieve for nothing, you desire nothing. The word *nothing* means "no thing." It's not a substance, but an atmosphere.

Through fear (which includes desire), you get into a movement of projecting from the past into the future. So sneaking around the spiritual ego means the ending of projection, so that you do not want anything, not even enlightenment. Wanting to be enlightened is the barrier to enlightenment. We simply want to be in touch with the climate, the third part of feelings. The ego and the thoughts dissolve once you are in touch with the climate.

FEEDING THE CLIMATE

What Ashtavakra says about stillness has to do with not nourishing fast feelings, as fast feelings will bring you to thoughts. Do not even nourish the slow feelings, because they too bring you to thoughts. You cannot hang onto this third state of feelings, as it is a cycle of coming and going. It is a wave. Look at the whole. Nourish the climate.

In psychotherapy we try to help clients not to focus on their fast feelings, or on their history of depression, or on their slow feelings, or on anything else that is troubling them. We help them into connection with their climate, but we can do this only if we, as therapists, are connected to our own own climate.

Ashtavakra says, at the end of the sutra, "The world with all its wonders is nothing." The mind is so convinced that if it can get out of the fast feeling state to be in contact with slow feelings, all will be well. Ashtavakra reminds us that this is still a wave, i.e., a form. You have to become the ocean in order to be in stillness. This is why he says the world with all its wonders is nothing, and when you know this, desire melts away. Once there is no more desire, and therefore no more fear, you are immediately connected with the climate. For you are awareness itself, he says.

If one is awareness itself, then there can be no one who is aware of the awareness.

The moment one has awareness of something, especially if it involves the mind comparing this with that, then attachment and clinging starts, and you lose the connection to the climate.

Stillness is the absence of clinging. When you know in your heart that there is nothing, you are still.

The easiest way to this stillness, to the climate, is to understand that whenever there is aggression it is a symptom of fear, and that this fear is a symptom of sadness, all of which arises out of the climate.

DROPPING INTO STILLNESS

Once you begin to see that all your feelings and thoughts arise out of the climate, and you don't focus too much on the outcome, but rather on the source, you naturally drop into stillness. Seeing everything as a ripple in the climate allows it all to fade away. As this integrates deeply in your heart, you will begin to be constantly connected to the climate, and stillness will follow as a natural process. In Time Therapy we say that the art of healing and of living is based on this third structure of feelings.

THE FIFTH SUTRA

*F*orget everything.

My child, you may read or discuss scriptures as much as you like,
but until you forget everything, you will never live in your heart.

You are wise, you play and work and meditate, but still your mind
desires that which is beyond everything,

Where all desires vanish, who is lazier than the master? He has
trouble even blinking, but only he is happy, no one else.

Seeing to this, neglecting that.

But when the mind stops setting one thing against another, it no
longer craves pleasure.

It no longer cares for wealth or religious duties or salvation.

Craving the pleasures or the senses, you suffer attachment,
disdaining them you learn detachment, but if you desire nothing
and disdain nothing, neither attachment nor detachment binds you.

If you desire liberation but you still say mine, if you feel you are the
body, you are not a wise man or a seeker; you are simply
a man who suffers.

Unless you forget everything, you will never live in your heart.

I LOVE ASHTAVAKRA BECAUSE HE GOES RIGHT TO THE ROOT
of knowing. How many books have we all read about love and
relationship, the cosmos, or how we should deal with each
other? Or the scriptures like the *Bhagavad Gita* or the
Upanishads? Have they made any difference to us?

Ashtavakra would probably say read on, but don't expect it
to change anything. To read a book or to listen to a talk in order

to grasp some new knowledge is useless; it is a waste of energy. However, there is immense value when you read to confirm your own observations.

There is no lack of good advice about new approaches to age-old problems in this world. Religions have told us how it should be, but the mind cannot respond to what should be. The mind finds itself split into should, must, and ought. The mind is never content with what it has seen, and like a junkie, it will always want to have more knowledge. This is because it believes that the more it knows, the better it will be, and the more intelligent it will become. Ashtavakra calls this absolute nonsense.

CREATING ILLUSION

Intelligence can arise only from your own observation. You may check to see if that observation is correct, through confirmation you get from what others have to say. Don't amass knowledge and then impose this on yourself. This will only create an illusion.

In the mystical sense illusions present themselves as visions, so when your awareness moves from the physical to the subtle there is always the danger that you will have visions, which may be nothing more than illusions.

For example, a Hindu mystic may have visions of Krishna, while a Christian may have visions of St. Francis of Assisi. These are pure illusion built up through knowledge, projected into space as desire.

Just as gathering knowledge is dangerous, so is there danger in this kind of vision, because it gives you the impression that you know something. What is really happening is that you are projecting certain forms of knowledge, or illusion, into space.

Over time, the difference between what is real and what is

projected fades, and it becomes difficult to distinguish between the two. Having a vision of the historical Buddha does not mean that you have become him or are in touch with him. This is similar to dreaming that you have won the lottery; it does not make you a millionaire. So be very careful about how you interpret visions. Ashtavakra's advice for avoiding the trap of visions and illusions would be to forget everything you have ever read or heard. You may read or discuss scriptures as much as you like, but until you forget everything you will never live in your heart. What exactly does he mean by forgetting everything?

LIVING IN THE HEART

When we habitually project knowledge into space, this creates the idea that we know something. When we are asked to forget this knowledge, we try to imagine that we never had it, and this is the wrong approach to the matter of forgetting. Ashtavakra is really saying that experience cannot be of value, and cannot be counted on when trying to move to a new level of consciousness, because all experience belongs to the past. By asking you to forget everything he is asking you to not cling to experiences.

Have you observed how the heart closes down once you begin to cling to an experience? For example, let's say you have experienced a person's love for you, therefore you project that experience into the future. It becomes an expectation, and if that person does not behave in the same way as in the previous experience, you feel hurt. The heart shuts down. Ashtavakra says every memory of an experience is clinging, attaching oneself to something in the past. This is how we create history.

Spirituality is about having the courage to die after every experience, and at the same time, retaining the capacity for memory in daily life. The ego depends on memory for survival in the material world and the brain is largely built on memory. Most psychotherapy is memory therapy. Spirituality is the ending of memory. Each has its place. There is nothing wrong with memory therapy, but this will help only to bring you to an understanding that there is something more than the ego, memory, and time.

Ashtavakra says that real spirituality has to do with the heart, and this goes beyond time. In Time Therapy our approach focuses on time – time being the ego. The point is to drop the ego and memory, and to touch the transcendental level.

BEYOND DESIRE

Ashtavakra goes on to say, "You are wise, you play and work and meditate, but still your mind desires that which is beyond everything, where all desire vanishes." Look at the beauty of this. This desire to go beyond everything is the place where all desire vanishes. Have a look at this in connection with the whole issue of experience.

Earlier we saw how it is not possible to work toward or perceive the state of enlightenment; we saw that once at the point of enlightenment, there is no sense of enlightenment. Similarly, going beyond desire leads to the vanishing of desire.

This presents a huge conflict, which you face when you drop into emptiness. All your experience vanishes once the memory is lost and the ego is transcended. What is left is "no experience," and in this state feelings are present, but you do not experience them. You are in the moment. If you were approached by anyone from the outside when you are in this state, the other person would experience the softness and feeling of love emanating from you, but *you* won't feel any of this. This is samadhi.

This is what Jesus meant when he used the word *innocence*. Innocence, in the spiritual context, does not mean that you become naïve and lose everything you know about the world, or turn your back on knowledge. To do this would be like throwing out the baby with the bathwater. Innocence, as Jesus uses it, means that you are not aware of your own beauty, of your own love.

This leads to another paradox that arises on this path. You need to have a certain degree of self-confidence at first. Initially, the spiritual ego needs to appreciate itself. It has to be able to see its own beauty as a first step, but then it has to step out of this self-awareness in order to bloom and not become corrupted.

Have you observed how you need a certain balance even in the area of being conscious? If you are too conscious of yourself, you will create distance around yourself because you will lose your relationship to the outside world. It is possible to be over-conscious of yourself and your actions and end up seeming unnatural or artificial.

According to Ashtavakra, enlightenment will happen only if you live in your heart. The heart here is a synonym for the point of no past or future. You cannot *work* at being with the heart. This happens only as a consequence of not clinging to experience. No one can describe this experience.

Living in the heart is about being in the zero factor, where you have knowledge, but you are not conscious of it. This is wisdom. A wise person does not go around selling her wisdom. A wise person does not think she has knowledge. A wise person is like a blind woman, walking through the mist of wisdom, where she can always attain more, and at the same time, she wants for nothing more.

Ashtavakra insists that none of this can happen if desire is present. The reason we read esoteric books and practice different styles of meditation is simply because we have desire. This is what he means by "but still your mind desires." He does not say "your mind desires" – the use of the word *but* implies *despite*. By using the word *still*, he means you are already engaged in something. So despite having reached a certain level of religiousness through understanding scriptures, and despite already being in the process of observing, you still experience desire.

FEAR AND DESIRE

In an earlier sutra Ashtavakra said that all sorrow comes from fear. In fact, fear and desire are twins. Desire is born out of fear – for example, I am afraid of this or that, therefore I desire to get out of this and that situation.

A huge part of consuming is related to this desire-fear axis. Desire can be built only upon experience, and to desire something, you need to have an experience of that something. Ashtavakra says you cannot live in the heart if you rely on experience.

Let me explain this to you very simply. To desire is like wanting to be present at your own funeral. You cannot be a witness (from a body-mind perspective) of your own funeral. As Ashtavakra says, you cannot meet God, you cannot experience God. If God is everything, how can you experience God?

To want to experience this requires that you split in two, and once you have done this, then you definitely cannot meet everything. Stillness is the ending of experience, and in that stillness the heart blossoms.

In this sutra Ashtavakra comes to another question: Who is lazier than a master? A master here means someone who has ceased to be attached, ceased to memorize, ceased to project experience into space. So Ashtavakra asks, who is lazier than the master, who has trouble even blinking? This is a beautiful symbol for the art of not doing. Ashtavakra claims that you cannot be in the climate, or the zero factor, or commune with God through doing.

A QUESTION OF MOTIVATION

Now the question arises: does being in touch with the climate require effortless awareness or does it require discipline? First, let's look at discipline.

Take the simple practical problem of brushing your teeth. Once you have developed an understanding of why you need to carry out this practice, does it then require discipline to brush your teeth every day? Both Ashtavakra and I would agree that it requires motivation rather than discipline.

When it comes to the question of spirituality, however, this motivational drive cannot be for your own sake, to improve your situation. It must be for the world, and not for yourself. This is what Jesus meant when he talked of serving and of compassion. Compassion is not something you attain through discipline. It's the pure motivation directed toward others.

How can you reach Brahma, Allah, Jehovah, God, or Buddhahood if the motivation is only for yourself? Whenever you do things for yourself you need discipline, but this will never bring you to the point of meeting the other dimension. The other dimension is like a huge door that opens only when your motivation is directed toward others. When you want to be enlightened in order to help others, and not yourself, then this door opens all by itself.

For Ashtavakra, discipline is nothing more than hard work. The master, remember, is too lazy to blink an eye. Motivation does not require the slightest effort. When you are motivated to do something, have you ever felt the burden of effort? Motivation brings you right to joy.

If you are motivated to win in a game, if you are motivated to study to become a doctor, these are personal goals for which you require discipline. Discipline is necessary on the material level, and there is nothing wrong with this. The motivation to better yourself materially can also help to provide the environment in which you can move on to the next level. However, once you are at the crossroads with the other dimension, the motivation must move naturally toward others.

FORGETTING THE SELF

Allow me to explain this by sharing a personal experience – call it enlightenment or whatever you choose. In June 1974, I was sitting in a room quietly, and then – whether it was an hour or a hundredth of a second, it's impossible to say – by just forgetting myself completely, without a trace of any sense of being in meditation, or even an awareness of sitting in the room, my whole structure changed. The feeling, the sensation of it, was as if a wave of energy had dissolved the whole body. The analyst Wilhelm Reich would probably have described it by saying it was as if the hard matter of the body had disappeared.

At that time I was working for Swiss radio, and the next morning my listeners called in complaining that I did not sound the same, and they didn't believe it was really me. My voice had totally changed. My whole structure had totally changed, and it could happen only because there was absolutely no trace of doing at the time. I have repeated this experience many times since, but never through doing anything. Through the exercise of doing I can change my material level of existence – improve my garden, for example – but the climate has never changed through an act of doing.

This, I believe, is what Ashtavakra meant when he used the word laziness, but the difficulty here is that being lazy is a form of doing. How do you stop doing anything any more? Trying not to do anything is, in fact, a terrible effort!

This is why in Christianity the word *grace* is used to describe enlightenment. It is a description of a combination of trust and of not being aware of what's happening. In Ashtavakra's terms we would call it no experience. Grace means that you cannot achieve this for yourself. All one can do is to be receptive, like a mother is toward her child. In fact it's quite simple. Good parenting means you are always receptive, without manipulating the child, and you are always present to take over when it is necessary. You should leave a lot of space for the child to find his or her own way in the intervening time.

In another sutra, Ashtavakra says, "It is a prison to practice samadhi." Even more precisely, he says, it is *your* prison to practice samadhi. Every act of practice creates an experience, and this experience becomes the barrier to samadhi.

EFFORTLESS AWARENESS

Another question Ashtavakra addresses is related to effortless awareness. Effortless awareness is not difficult. It is not difficult to be aware of the climate. If you observe carefully you will find that it is actually much more difficult to follow a thought and a feeling than to observe or to be aware of space.

I believe this is so because we are observation in our very nature. Observation is like breathing in and out; it is always present. It does not require any effort. Effort, however, is needed to follow a thought and to understand the content of the thought.

This is why we cling to a thought and try to extract meaning out of it. The thought in itself has no meaning. You have one thought, and then another thought comes in to give that first thought a description, and then there may be another thought that is a description to verify if the first description is correct. So you need at least three or four thoughts just to understand one thought. This requires huge effort and to me seems a terrible waste of energy.

Don't bother to cling to thoughts or try to understand them or try to give them a sense of identity. Just be there. Observation happens anyway. In clinging to thoughts, I separate myself from the observer, and there is no need to do this. You are observation and observer at the same time, and as a result of this you fall into effortless awareness. The mind insists on observing specific things, and so the mind is awareness with effort.

Let us imagine that you are sitting in a field with hundreds of flowers around you. Awareness with effort would be trying to figure out what each flower is and comparing one flower with another. You interpret whatever you see and describe its color; you even have the thought of whether or not it is beautiful. This is awareness with effort.

On the other hand, you can just sit, watching the whole field of flowers, and soak up its atmosphere. This does not require the slightest effort of awareness. We are a field of flowers; don't focus on individual flowers, just look at the whole.

When Ashtavakra says "Seeing to this, neglecting that, once the mind stops setting one thing against another, it no longer craves pleasure," he is referring to how the mind is always drawing comparisons, and therefore creating effort in awareness.

As long as the mind is focusing on specific things, it cannot see the whole. You will always have one thought chasing after the other to see if it's a good or a bad thought, and so on and so forth.

Consequently, you end up clinging to the thought. You then miss the natural free awareness of observation of the climate.

The mind always hopes to get enlightened by grasping more understanding from the scriptures and books and the practice of meditation, hoping that by doing this it can direct consciousness and reach enlightenment. The mind has ideas about enlightenment as a magical, special state of awareness, but let me remind you that this is never the case. If you believe this to be true you will be very disappointed when you become enlightened.

Remember the Zen master who said, "after enlightenment, roaring laughter," meaning that after enlightenment there is the recognition that there is nothing very special about it. It's your thoughts and feelings that lead you to the feeling of being something special.

All of this is what Ashtavakra would call illusion, a vision, which is a projection of desire. Buddha, meaning awake, is not something special. Enlightenment, the ending of the mind, is the ending of focusing on all thoughts and all feelings. The climate is a form of stillness and therefore is very natural and very simple. In this state, nothing feels special or out of the ordinary.

NOTHING SPECIAL

This is how the word *humbleness* comes about in Christian teaching. The mind tries to grasp this conceptually and then attempts to become humble. In doing this, the knowledge of humbleness gets projected into space and the illusion of humbleness is created. Humbleness simply means that once the mind is no longer dominant, there is nothing special present. It can even be a bit of a disappointment. When in 1974 my body, my mind, my spirit, whatever you may choose to call it, totally rearranged itself without any trace of me being there, there was no special feeling afterwards of ecstasy or a sense of being different. I just went about my life as usual.

Everything was just like it was before and yet it was totally different. However the difference was not something that could be experienced by me. This once again shows how innocence is so much a part of the whole process.

This is what Ashtavakra means when he says the prison you create for yourself is the exercising of samadhi. Observe how this goes hand in hand with the notion of experience. Exercising means discipline. Discipline requires that there must be a desire and an idea of what the end result is. No transformation can happen through having an experience projected as a desire into space.

SEEING THE WHOLE

Ashtavakra says, "Seeing to this, neglecting that, but when the mind stops setting one thing against the other it no longer cares for wealth or religious duty or salvation." Think about the beauty of this. Once you have stopped focusing, attaching to a thought, to a God or to a projection of your experience, there is this peace. Who then needs to deal with religion, duties, or salvation?

In Time Therapy we say that a problem has nothing to do with having a weakness, but rather with the desire to observe the weakness, which is exactly like trying to become enlightened. Enlightenment is not about focusing either on the weakness or on something positive. If you focus too much on what's good, you merely become arrogant. Enlightenment is about looking at the whole; it is not about doing any one thing. It is about having the motivation to be there for others.

Any weakness can be a strong force of energy, if only you do not act against it by wanting to be rid of it. Wanting to get rid of your weakness implies that the motivation is directed toward yourself, toward wanting to become a better person. When you are present for the purpose of helping others in the world, this weakness suddenly disappears by itself.

Having weaknesses does not mean that you are unable to love. For example, Hitler was a perverse psychopath, but had you been close to him, as Eva Braun was, you would have seen a man who was able to love. Be very careful not to fall into the trap of psychology by thinking that someone who is bad is not able to love. Bad actions and love can go together very easily.

The mind creates the image that someone bad is not able to love, as it can't bear to think of someone who is capable of doing evil also being loving. So abide by what Ashtavakra says and do not set one thing against another. It is very dangerous not to see the whole picture, and this is most dangerous when we fail to see the whole picture of ourselves.

According to Ashtavakra, you will never live in your heart until you forget everything, including the most penetrating scriptures. For example, Jung claimed that we each have a shadow – parts of ourselves we find unacceptable. He wanted us to work through the shadow, meaning simply to acknowledge it as part of ourselves. The shadow is part of you, so don't try to get rid of it, because in doing this you only destroy the heart. Wanting to get rid of the shadow is like wanting to have day without night. I'm convinced the so-called badness of a person surfaces because they are fighting a part of themself instead of accepting it.

When you split yourself in two, the good and the bad, you create conflict in yourself, which can bring on psychopathic reactions. But it is the conflict, not the shadow itself, that creates the psychopathic reaction. It's the constant fighting with oneself that takes us away from our true nature. Ashtavakra insists that a master is someone who is even too lazy to blink an eyelid, or care about religion, duties, or salvation. Is it not simply enough to have effortless awareness in the motivation to be there for the world, to just be the nature of observation?

ATTACHMENT TO DETACHING

People often ask me what I did to enable the transformation that took place. All I can remember about what preceded the experience was that I was terribly bored. I was sitting in the room, not even consciously meditating, just simply sitting there, because there was nothing for me to do. I did not fight that boredom; I was able to just leave it alone.

In Ashtavakra's terms, this is forgetting everything. By asking us to forget everything, he is also asking us to forget ourselves. Just a second of not bothering about yourself is all that is required. Once there, you don't even have an awareness of being in the process of observation. The crazy thing is that it is not possible for this to happen while practicing meditation. I see meditation as a tool to lead you to the climate where boredom can become so great that you drop into a state of stillness, forgetting everything.

When he says "craving the pleasure of the senses, you suffer attachment," Ashtavakra means that you long for the experiences of the body, the thoughts, and the feelings. The desire to experience yourself creates attachment. It is very important to understand this: attachment is the movement of trying to get a sense of yourself, while being in samadhi. Allah, God, Brahman, or Buddha is the absence of the self, the ending of experience.

Attachment arises as a result of the desire to have an orientation, the longing for the experience of the self, of "I am." You cannot detach consciously from yourself, because to want to detach is a movement of doing. The I would have to do the detaching, therefore it does not really detach. All it does is to create an attachment to detachment!

As Ashtavakra says, "Disdaining them, you learn detachment." Here you get a taste of detachment by not caring about having a sense of yourself. However, this is not the path to true detachment. Ashtavakra keeps returning to the problem of desire, because herein lies the path to detachment. "If you desire nothing and disdain nothing, neither attachment nor detachment binds you." Remember that desire is created by fear, and all suffering comes out of fear.

So it's not about attachment or detachment. It's either, nothing, or both. The heart is incapable of having any feeling of attachment or detachment. The heart in this sense is neutral. On the level of spirituality, the word neutral refers to stillness. This also explains why there is an absence of feelings when you are connected to the climate. When you are neutral, there are no feelings, not because there are no feelings as such, but because there is no experiencer present.

Going back to the example of the ocean and the waves, the waves are the feelings or thoughts. Thoughts and feelings can never be separated. Observe carefully that when a feeling is present there is also a description of the feeling arising out of thought. The absence of thoughts and feelings is enlightenment, and at this moment there is no experiencer to describe any of this.

Let's say you are swimming in the ocean, bobbing up and down with the waves. This would represent your awareness. You then plunge down deeper into the water and find there is calmness. There are no longer any waves, just still water, and you're just down there in silence. You are still aware that it is water, but the description of the water derives from the waves and the water does not have a form, therefore you cannot describe it. The Sufi master Rumi says that once the wave realizes that it is a wave of the ocean, it becomes the ocean.

You must have met people who give the impression that they have absolutely no feelings. When you ask them how they feel, you get a blank look. This doesn't mean that they have no feelings; it is just that their feelings are translated very quickly into thoughts. Remember that thoughts and feelings cannot be separated. Such people may not be able to express a feeling, but there is a constant flow of thoughts, so you have to trace their thoughts back to feelings.

The only way to tell if you are really in the climate is to check and see if you have lots of thoughts. If there is no feeling, but thought is present, then thought has blocked the energy of feelings.

Initially your experience of the climate is like a pulsation, so it won't be present continuously. You will find that it comes, vanishes, and returns, because the mind is not used to this new state. When you dive and you go down deep into the water, you need to come up for air; you then take a breath, and you go down again. This same movement takes place when you first come into contact with the climate, until you are able to remain calm in doing nothing.

DESIRING LIBERATION

Ashtavakra then goes on to say that if you desire liberation but you still say *mine* – if you feel you are the body – you are not a wise man or a seeker. Now this brings us back to motivation. Discipline comes out of "me wanting to do something for me." In this case, I want to reach a state of liberation, but there is this ugly business of hierarchies and notions of superiority and its accompanying spiritual elitism.

Ashtavakra points out that this is precisely the trap. The motivation should be not me for me, but me for the world – the motivation should be about *we*. He says the problem is not what you think or feel, or whether you have a certain amount of knowledge – the problem is the me in all of this. If you desire liberation but you keep saying mine, then it's no longer liberation. Liberation is the ending of the mine, and the mind.

With the ending of the mind, there is no longer anyone experiencing liberation. The me who wants to experience liberation cannot be free. And as long as you feel you are the body (meaning the body-mind with all its inputs), you are not a wise man or a seeker. Even a seeker has to stop being in the mind.

What is the first level of me? To use the ocean metaphor again, we might say that before enlightenment, each wave when it sees itself separated from the ocean thinks it is something different from the water or the ocean. This is equivalent to the me part of ourselves. So each thought and feeling, even the fast and the slow feelings, are a description of me. They are the experience of me. This is not liberation.

Remember that every effort creates a sense of the me. The heart functions best through forgetting everything, says Ashtavakra. So the first thing to do is to not care about thoughts and feelings, as these give identification to the me. Releasing concern about this takes away the process of identification.

The next step relates to the climate. The climate is personal, but it is something that is not possible to identify with. Thoughts and feelings may be identified with, but one cannot identify with atmosphere. Let's take the pragmatic example of going into a church. In the church you may identify with the cross and Jesus hanging on it. You can identify with a bouquet of flowers or candles, but the climate of the church is some-thing you just feel without any identification, despite the fact that there is still a personal dimension to belonging to a church.

Just before one dies, the person has an atmosphere made up of a quality, which is impersonal, and a climate. If you relate to the person based on their feelings and thoughts, you don't actually know them. If you look at their climate, you know the person. This is especially evident in dying. Once a person dies you will still feel the atmosphere, however the climate is now gone. That's why the climate is personal – it belongs to the person who has radiated that climate, but it is not identified with them. That's why I make the distinction between climate and atmosphere. The quality, the atmosphere of a person who has died, is present for a long time after death. The climate, how-ever, ends with death.

As Ashtavakra says, if you desire liberation, stop dealing with the mind. The Buddha said it differently – that enlighten-ment is the ending of identification. Only thoughts and fast and slow feelings can be identified with. You can never identi-fy with the atmosphere; you cannot say this is my atmosphere. Climate cannot be identified with, but you can feel it even though you cannot grasp it as your own.

WORKING WITH THE HEART

In Time Therapy, the out-of-body consciousness is anchored over the heart, rooted in the heart. If we take away the symbol-ic meaning, then the heart in fact means the part of the being that is not oriented toward a thought or a feeling. Because it is always present, you need much less effort to observe the part unrelated to thoughts and feelings.

Most of these thoughts and feelings are manipulated from the outside – whatever comes into your view creates a thought, so most thoughts are not even one's own thoughts. And to cling to something that is not part of the eternal and is vanishing quickly is a waste of energy.

Ashtavakra calls all this an illusion, an experience projected into space. If you observe carefully, you will see that 80 percent of our thoughts and feelings are not created by our own free will. They are in fact reactions to what we see on the outside. This is what the scientist Benjamin Libet meant when he talked about the so-called free will. What is the point of giving so much importance to our reactions to the outside?

But despite all of this, even if the outside triggers all these reactions of thoughts and feelings within us, there is still a central part – our climate – that is constantly independent of them. And resting here is what Ashtavakra refers to as working with the heart.

THE SIXTH SUTRA

The clear space of awareness.

You are not your body, your body is not you.

You are not the doer, you are not the enjoyer.

You are pure awareness, the witness of all things.

You are without expectation, free.

Wherever you go, be happy.

Desire and aversion are of mind, the mind is never yours.

You are free of its turmoil.

You are awareness itself, never changing.

Wherever you go, be happy, for, see, the self is in all beings, and all beings are in the self.

Know you are free, free of I, free of mine; be happy.

In you the worlds arise like waves in the sea.

It is true, you are awareness itself, so free yourself from the fever of the world.

If the body lasted till the end of time or vanished today, what would you win or lose?

You are pure awareness, you are the endless sea in whom all the worlds, like waves, naturally rise and fall.

You have nothing to win, nothing to lose.

Child, you are pure awareness, nothing else.

You and the world are one, so who are you to think you can hold on to it or let it go, how could you?

You are the clear space of awareness, pure and still, in whom there is no birth, no activity, no I.

You are one and the same, you cannot change or die.

The world only arises from ignorance, you alone are real.

There is no one, not even God, separated from yourself.

You are pure awareness; the world is an illusion, nothing more.

When you understand this fully desire falls away, you find peace, for indeed there is nothing.

In the ocean of being there is only one, there was and there will be only one.

You are already fulfilled, how can you be bound or free?

Wherever you go, be happy.

Never upset your mind with yes or no.

Be quiet, you are awareness itself.

Live in the happiness of your own nature, which is happiness itself.

What is the use of thinking?

Once and for all, give up meditation, hold nothing in your mind.

You are the self and you are free.

IN TWO SENTENCES, ASHTAVAKRA DESTROYS THE WHOLE philosophical concept of eastern religions. Once and for all, he says at the end of the sutra, give up meditation; hold nothing in your mind. Meditation, he says, is part of the mind, an experience carried out by the mind. He even goes so far as to say, you are already fulfilled, so how can you be bound or free?

For thousands of years, the practice of meditation has been promoted as the technique to lead you to freedom. Ashtavakra says that through meditating you are creating the illusion that you are becoming free, but as you are already free, you are pushing against an open door. You are awareness itself, and the practice of meditation is taking the awareness away, like creating artificial clouds in a sky that is already blue.

Notice that Ashtavakra does not say stop meditating; he says when you understand that you are pure awareness, the world is nothing more than an illusion. So once you understand that, stop meditating. The moment you grasp this, there is no need for meditation, because then meditation becomes a prison.

As we saw earlier, the moment you make an experience of enlightenment, there is no longer any sense of enlightenment. Enlightenment is the absence of the experience of enlightenment. Ashtavakra says that once you see that, there is pure awareness; one is pure awareness, so what is the use of thinking?

If you observe the process of thinking very carefully, you can see that it is like a map for the mind. Thinking does not create anything new. It's a map to help you negotiate your way through life. Ashtavakra says, who needs a map, who needs negotiation, who needs direction when there is pure awareness? There is nowhere to go. There is neither yes nor no. Be quiet, be still. In the ocean of being there is only one.

A map is there to help us move from one point to another. The mind map, or thinking, helps us to move from one part to another, to be oriented. But pure awareness does not move anywhere. It is a presence. It has arrived. The conceptual meaning of the Buddha's word *enlightenment* is that there is nowhere to go. You have arrived, you are Buddhahood, and Buddhahood is always present.

HAPPINESS ITSELF

Note the tremendous depth of what Ashtavakra is saying here. Live in the happiness of your own nature, which is happiness itself. Listen with your feelings, with your whole being, to these simple sentences that contain the whole truth of the universe. Live in the happiness of your own nature, which is happiness itself. Note that he is not telling us to *be* happy or reassuring us that when we find happiness everything will be perfect. Our true nature is not separate from the simple fact of our being alive.

You are happiness, says Ashtavakra. This does not mean "I have happiness." The slow feeling of "I am happy" is a different story from the climate of happiness. The atmosphere is happiness. Not I have, I am, not just a description of happiness, but pure and simple happiness. There are no more boundaries between my happiness and your happiness. Our true nature is simply happiness.

When you have reached where you wanted to go, you don't cling to the map. The personality, the map, has disappeared. In Ashtavakra's words, what is the use of thinking?

When you are there once and for all, he says, give up meditation. Meditation is a spiritual map. But a spiritual map tells us only that there is separation between the me and the spiritual.

In fact, Ashtavakra is dealing with one of the biggest mistakes of modern psychology. As we saw earlier, all suffering comes out of fear. To understand how psychology went wrong, we have to understand how fear comes into being. Remember also that fear creates desire for escape, to be better, or whatever it is we feel we should be doing. How does fear come into being?

CREATING FEAR

Ashtavakra insists, as does the Buddha (who said you are always and will never be anything other than Buddha nature), that one is never separated. As he says, you are not even separated from God. There is no one, not even God, separated from you. He insists that you are always, even with your strangest attitudes and behaviors, part of the One. So if that's how it is for all of us, how does fear come into being?

Fear is always created by the illusion, by the idea that you have to *become* – that something about you has to change. In the Christian tradition, for example, you are born as a sinner, which means that from the beginning you are in fact not as you *should* be. Each human being is a huge *should*, and that's the fundamental mistake.

Psychology starts with the idea that you were constantly manipulated in your childhood, that your parents were constantly manipulated in their childhood, and that therefore you are nothing else than a manipulated structure that has to change. In spiritual terminology, you have to become enlightened to be good.

In the main religious traditions – Christianity, Buddhism, Islam, and Hinduism – what is the basic pattern? In Christianity we have the Sermon on the Mount, or the Ten Commandments. In Buddhism we have the Four Noble Truths and the Eightfold Path. Islamic law, as set out in the *Koran*, covers public and personal life. In Hinduism the teachings of the *Bhagavad Gita* give instruction on how one should conduct oneself. They all have in common guidelines such as you shouldn't lie, you shouldn't be violent, you should respect all people, especially your parents, and so on.

Not one of them is saying you should behave according to these rules because you are bad – they just suggest trying not to lie, trying not to cheat, trying not to kill, because it makes life easier. They don't say you are a killer and you should stop being a killer; change, and then you will no longer be a bad person. None of them insists that something is fundamentally wrong with you and therefore you should change. They just set out ethical and moral codes of practice based on how much better it would be if you didn't cheat, if you didn't lie, and if you weren't violent.

Over the last hundred years psychology has taught us that now it is not only a question of *not* lying, cheating, or killing for the common good, but that unconsciously we constantly want to cheat, lie, and kill. Consciously and unconsciously, according to modern psychology, we are the way we are because of how we were manipulated in childhood. You have to seek out why you are bad, because you have no consciousness about your badness. Once you have seen that, you may become a better person. What else can that sort of conditioning produce but fear? The idea that everything you do, you do unconsciously, not only destroys your dignity, it creates a tremendous amount of fear.

This is all in complete contrast to the teachings of the Buddha and of Ashtavakra. They say our basic nature is good, but at the same time it's helpful to have some guidelines on how to live our lives. Of course if you realize that you are bad and maybe part of it is unconscious, your fear becomes even stronger. You then become desperate to escape the fear.

What's the first thing that happens when someone is fearful? They attach themselves to someone whom they think is less fearful. There must be someone somewhere to guide me, to help me get out of this fear. I cannot manage this by myself, so I have to give myself up to someone who perceives more clearly than I do – priests, gurus, absurd authorities from outer space, angels, or spirits. We then start to cling to authorities and we lose ourselves even more.

Whenever you cling to an authority, you create even more

fear in yourself. Not only is there the fear that you are bad, and you don't know how to escape from your badness, but also that the authority will one day drop you, or not love you, which will prove that you are really very, very bad.

Psychological fear is not innate. It is simply built on the idea that I have to become different than I am. Every day I realize I change a little, but I cannot really change fundamentally. If you were able to change fundamentally, you would be a different person from the one you are, and I would call that psychosis.

Your body constantly changes from birth till death. Your thinking, the map you use for guidance, changes according to your age. But there is a part that you always know as your self – the climate, the atmosphere, the qualities. That is never going to change.

Let's take three examples of how you may think you have to change. 1) I can't be spiritual if I am sexual. 2) I won't become enlightened if I occasionally get angry. 3) I'm sure something is wrong with me; I have a fear of not being loved.

These feelings never go away, and there's constantly an energy of fear – the fear of not being able to change. It is the fear that makes you constantly want to change, but the change is never going to happen. You may have had the worst childhood or the best childhood. This is independent from the feeling chain of aggression as a symptom of fear, and fear as a symptom of sadness. It is independent from feelings of joy, happiness, and love.

A childhood in a bad foster home, for example, will give you another input in the chain reaction of fear. Perhaps you will resort to fast feelings more readily than someone who was treated differently. If you had a so-called unhappy childhood, the fear that you have to become different is stronger and even more penetrating than if you had a good one. In your nature, however, you're not going to change.

That's what Ashtavakra is constantly getting back to. The world arises only from ignorance. You alone are real. Observe! The world arises only from ignorance. The fear that we have to change becomes so strong that we have created concepts of how it will be when we have changed – how it will be when we are good, enlightened, a holy person. Then comes a whole chain of assumptions about how a holy person looks and how a holy person should be. I remember when Jesudian, a wonderful Indian person who taught yoga for years in Zurich, suddenly married a very nice, simple Swiss girl called Vreni. Many of his women followers fell into a deep depression – this spiritual man marrying a normal Swiss girl! What has happened to him?

We create endless descriptions of how it will be when we are perfect, and the descriptions are so extreme that even if it were possible to change we would never manage it. Ashtavakra says this is the ignorance of the world. This is the separation between good and bad. He says there is no one, not even God, separated from you. There is no separation between good and bad.

Start to fight your weaknesses and you set out on a path to trouble. You will only create more fear.

Sit in meditation, visualize how it should be, build up an expectation – and what happens when you don't change? You become more blocked in your brain. You say, well, something is wrong, I haven't managed to succeed in this, and it should be different. What does that ignorance create – that separation between how it should be and how it is? It creates fear! The fear that I still cannot succeed, I'm still not good enough, I'm a failure.

Ashtavakra reminds us that we are pure awareness; there is

no separation between good and bad. When there is pure awareness, he says, it means that the world is an illusion, nothing more. Not the philosophical concept of illusion, which means that the world is happening only in your head – he means simply the illusion that things can be separated. In its true nature, the energy of aggression is just energy; what makes it destructive or not is the way that you direct it.

The energy that can be expressed as aggression is the same energy that can be used as love. So to repress it and say that energy is bad in one case and good in the other, Ashtavakra says, is an illusion. When you understand this fully, desire falls away.

The mistake of psychology, therefore, is the idea that you need to change, which gives rise to a constant desire to be different than you are. It's precisely that desire to be different that creates the conflict, and therefore more fear.

THE EGO IS LIKE THE APPLE

Imagine a beautiful apple tree in the spring. Along comes a psychologist or a priest (in times gone by priests were the psychologists) and he says, "This is not what you are here for, apple tree. You must have apples! Where are the apples?" The apple tree starts to shiver, and says, "I'm so sorry, I am wasting my energy, I will do my best to have apples. But how do I do that?" The priest says, "Become a Christian or a Hindu, meditate, begin spiritual exercises." Or the therapist says, let's go back and see how your parents were and if they had apples. It is very difficult to find out if they had apples. So the apple tree starts to work. Energy work, exercises, meditation. And still in June, no apples. That creates more frustration. I want apples; to have apples means enlightenment. I want to have apples!

And now, imagine that one day in autumn the apples

appear! It's a natural process. The tree could have stayed just as it was. All those exercises didn't help at all; all that fear was a waste of energy. The apples will appear one day anyway, they will be around for a while, and then they will fall from the tree.

If the tree falls into the trap of psychology, it will start the cycle all over again. I have no apples! What's wrong with me, why have they fallen down, shouldn't there be apples all the time? Ashtavakra tells us they are always there, but sometimes they are present in a form, while at other times they are hidden in the seed.

The caterpillar who gets frustrated because it's not a butterfly can never experience itself being the butterfly; it has to die to become the butterfly. It will be in constant fear of not having reached its butterfly form; it will fight and work to succeed, but this does not change anything.

The human universe is like a closed flower that starts to unfold. The only thing that prevents that from happening naturally is trying to force it. Trying to do it, to become it, to control how and when the unfolding should happen is the illusion – in the words of Ashtavakra, the world arises only from ignorance. The apple tree is constantly full of the potential for apples! That's enough; the apples will appear in their own time.

Ashtavakra was being compassionate in telling us to give up meditation. Stop trying to grow! It's trying to grow that creates the illusion of not seeing the potential in your *being* the apple tree. What would apples do without the tree? Is it not much holier and more spiritual to produce a fair crop of apples every year than to try for one big apple that puts an end to the movement of life? The apple tree in spring without apples is more productive, because substance from the blossom returns to the ground to nourish growth; so new apple trees are born when the tree is blossoming, much before the apple appears. It's not the result that counts but the natural rhythm in which things don't just happen once, but continue in a constant returning and renewing of the cycle – a recognition of the whole.

Enlightenment is not one unique experience and then it's finished. That's what Ashtavakra means when he says there is no separation. Fighting against one's weaknesses creates identification with the weakness, imprisonment in the weakness. Ashtavakra says you are the clear space of awareness, pure and still, in whom there is no birth, no activity, no I. The apple tree and the apples are the I. That is the outcome. There is nothing wrong with the I, with the ego. It is fighting against the ego that is the problem.

TRANSFORMATION THROUGH OBSERVATION

The ego is the apple. Eat it, swallow it, and go on. Reaching is not the solution. Ashtavakra insists you are one and the same, you cannot change or die. This is beautiful. The apple falls from the tree after it appears. Whether it's eaten or not eaten doesn't make any difference to the apple. The apple falling from the tree is the dying process; the tree, as a symbol for consciousness, is not going to die because of this, just as the ocean is not going to die because a wave comes and goes. The wave, as beautiful as it may be in the water, is going to die. Therefore, enlightenment is not dependent on changing the state of the I, the ego.

The color, shape, and size of the apples the tree produces may change from year to year. It's the atmosphere of the apple tree, the strength, the blossoming of the apple tree that counts, like the unfolding and closing of a rose. That's what it's all about. So, therefore, there is no need to change.

If there is nothing that can be changed, then what is left is stillness. Stillness is nothing other than observing whatever is there without any concept that it has to be different. Be very careful with the concept that you have to be different than you are. There is absolutely nothing wrong with aggression as long you observe it, because observation transforms aggression. There is absolutely nothing wrong with jealousy or greed as long as you observe it, and the observation then transforms it.

Whenever you fight against your aggression it means you have created a split, and there will not be sufficient energy for observation and transformation.

Again, modern psychology is responsible for the belief that we have to struggle with the unconscious. How can there be peace and stillness if you fight? How can aggression be transformed to pure energy if you resist and react to it?

Aggression against aggression leads only to aggression, as Krishnamurti and other great souls have said. They were not talking about the condition of the outside world. Fighting against your weakness will create more weakness. You can analyze the weakness as much as you want, it will not change a single bit. It will create ignorance – the illusion that you are different.

OFF THE MAP

The difference between you as you are now and your state of being is not dependent on understanding why you are aggressive. The difference depends on whether or not you can be in stillness. If you suddenly become non-aggressive but continue to think in the same way, this simply means that you have invested your energy into trying to hold back.

Jesus was so totally misunderstood when he said that even if you just think of betraying your wife, you have in effect already betrayed your wife. Have you ever grasped the beauty of this? Since thinking is the map of orientation in this world, you can control energy by thinking. Energy follows thought. When you think of betraying your wife and another thought is holding you back from doing it, says Jesus, you have already cheated, because to think about it is the same as actually doing it.

Thoughts control energy, so whether I use the energy or not it amounts to the same thing. Only stillness makes a difference. Krishna goes even further. Krishna says to Arjuna in the *Gita*, whatever you see as spirits, as ideas, are created by your thoughts – it's Maya. Only when there is absolutely nothing – the oneness of Ashtavakra, the stillness – are you different. You are still the same, but you are different. All the rest is just about creating an illusion.

One is not a more loving person because one is not aggressive. The aggression may come up any moment that the mind, thoughts, cannot hold it back and control it enough. It is this idea of having to change that has created hell on earth. The Muslim thinks the Christian should change to become a Muslim, and the same Muslim thinks he has to follow the law of the *Koran* exactly, otherwise he is not good enough, he is not religious. In many ways, the Christian and the Buddhist think the same. We are prisoners of maps and concepts. We do not walk in our true nature, we follow the map.

And Ashtavakra says, whether the body lasts till the end of time or vanishes today, what would you win or lose either way? You are pure awareness. Don't forget, he is referring to the mind and the physical body. If the apple falls from the tree, what does the tree lose? The apple tree is the source and in its being cannot change. One year it may have more apples, the next year fewer, but it's not going to alter its essence. You have nothing to win, nothing to lose. Look at these two sentences together: You have nothing to win and nothing to lose; you are one and the same, you cannot change or die.

We are constantly chasing ideas of how we should be. This is not spirituality. Spirituality is the end of chasing, fighting, wanting to be different than you are. You have nothing to win, nothing to lose; therefore, all this growing and changing is a waste of effort.

Imagine doing seven hours of tai chi or eight hours of meditation every day for thirty years, fighting with your body and your mind to get it exactly right – and what happens? There are constant battles with yourself, and there is fear. Whenever there is fear, it's a beautiful sign that you are against yourself. Fear is not a rational construction. There is nothing to be afraid of but your battle against yourself. Fear shows you that you have split the energy in two – me against something different. You have lost the connection with the apple tree. You have isolated the apple from the tree. You are looking at a rose that has not yet unfolded, and you are cutting the rosebud – but then it will never unfold.

Once more: You are the clear space of awareness, pure and still, in whom there is no birth, no activity, no I. You are one and the same, you cannot change or die. Let's take "or die" away. Let's say this is a desire, wishful thinking, because none of us knows what really happens after we are dead. Let's keep it on a level that we can observe ourselves. Let's keep it on the level where I can see if I have changed.

We have rearranged concepts, which means we have taken one map and replaced it with another map. Is that change? We have learned to control our behavior using the map, or thinking, as a tool. Is that change?

We have learned through our analytical process to be more

at peace with ourselves. But a little peace in ourselves – is that change? The mind says, yes, that's the problem, we still haven't changed enough, so let's make more effort, let's try some more. Ashtavakra and Time Therapy say, no, stop it, there is no need to change.

Love does not depend on your attitude. Love does not depend on understanding things. Love does not depend on becoming different. Stop all this effort. Each effort means war with yourself. Desire and aversion are of the mind. The mind is never yours. You are free of its turmoil.

Is there anything in our mind that comes from us? In Time Therapy we say the mind is a broken mirror. Imagine a mirror on which you paint beautiful colors – turquoise, purple, gold, or dark blue. You create a lovely picture, not with forms, just colors. Every day, depending on what state of mind you are in when you look at the mirror, you first look a bit more at one color, and then more at another color, according to your preference, which comes out of your emotional state that day, or out of your so-called unconscious. You don't even know why today you're more attracted to blue, and another day it's the purple. Some would identify your psychological state from this preference – for example, blue because you are feeling calm, red because you are feeling angry, and so on.

Ashtavakra says you can identify with all these colors and you can say this is mine, until you see through it all and the mirror breaks. It is shattered into thousands of pieces, millions of little dots of colors on the floor. It shatters when you realize that the entire mind is constantly rearranged according to what Ashtavakra calls the illusion, the unreality of the world. But we are not the mirror. We are not the mind, he says. You are awareness itself, never changing. That cannot be broken. You do not identify with different colors, you are beyond that.

Let's take a simple example. Say you grew up in a Christian environment in the West, over the last twenty years. You may have had a phase when you were really beginning to believe in Christianity. Then one day you realized somehow that it no longer satisfies you. You become disappointed, and instead of taking this tremendous chance to go into total insecurity, without any possibility of trying another new map, you switch to Buddhism. You start to read the Buddhist texts, perhaps you even convert to Buddhism, or to Sufism, or any other 'ism. All of this is a constant escape from your true nature. You know that somewhere under the scriptures, under the rituals, under the descriptions there is something that endures and is unrelated to all of this.

Love is not stronger in Buddhism than in Christianity or in Islam. You are awareness itself, not a concept in a religion. Buddha was never a Buddhist. As he said, "I am simply awake," which is the true meaning of the word *Buddha*.

THE IDENTIFICATION GAME

Never changing, the mind can play the game of change as much as it wants – a beautiful, playful game. But what is playfulness? Everything is energy, so you have to look at processes from the energy level.

What is the energy level of playfulness? To be pl.ayful is to use items without identifying with them or with the experience. All children do this. What do we do? We start looking at meditation in playfulness, and then we start to get serious with our effort and we cling to our practice. The playfulness is gone, because we have identified with the practice. When two children play with a toy and then begin to identify with it, the playfulness disappears, and they start to fight about who should have the toy.

Playfulness can move to war very quickly. But playfulness in itself is a useful tool of the mind. I must repeat that there's nothing wrong with the ego, the mind. The mind is a beautiful instrument, but it has to keep its playfulness, never taking *what is* as the complete truth. The Buddha's teachings are beautiful, but to go and sit every day for years and repeat a mantra is pure stupidity – there is no playfulness here. Once the identification process has started, desire comes up. Desire is in fact the energy movement of a feeling deep down of frustration and the hope of escaping the frustration. That's what desire is. Frustration, in its essence, is fear.

Ashtavakra says, "Never changing [as you can never change], wherever you go, be happy." He doesn't mean wherever you go in your travels; he is talking about your inner space. If you cannot change, there is no point in making an effort to be different and in the process losing your playfulness.

Whenever you try to use a technique, a substance, an idea to reach some goal, it will hold you back. It will create opposition. The same thing happens when you are in a relationship. The easiest way to destroy a relationship is to ask the other to be different from how she or he is. How can you call it love to ask the other to be different than they are? I'm sure you would agree that's not love. If you start to ask the other to change, you had better end the relationship.

CAN THE CLIMATE CHANGE?

Now what about oneself? Both religion and psychology have given you the idea that you have to be different. Can I have a good relationship with myself if I constantly think that I have to change? To make matters worse, I don't even know exactly how I need to be different. I have only some ideas about it.

So, says Ashtavakra, "For, see, the self is in all beings and all beings are in the self." Know you are free, free of I, free of mine. He does not say be free from aggression. He does not say be free from weakness. He says simply, be free from I and mine. See that there is no change possible. (The I you can change a little, but even that's an illusion.) Your source, the apple tree – which is what you are – fundamentally is never going to change.

So why bother? Why make a fuss? In you, the world arises like waves in the sea. Ashtavakra reminds us constantly that the concept of the world is arising within us like waves in the sea. Let concepts remain, as that's part of playfulness, but don't start to confuse the wave, or the concept, with the ocean.

You all know the Zen master's saying, "When I point my finger at the moon, don't look at the finger." The finger is simply the map – look at the moon! And when you look at the moon, Ashtavakra says, you are aware of the sun at the same time. Since there would be no moon without the sun, the moon must remind you of the sun.

Let's take another question: does the climate change? Ashtavakra says nothing changes. What is the energy aspect of change? In our simple example, look at an apple tree when there is absolutely no wind, and then when it gets windy. You see a difference; in the wind, you see and hear the leaves begin to rustle and the apples move. If the tree's in blossom, the blossoms fly away.

Change is movement. Now imagine the waves on a windy day. The waves represent the I; the climate is the deep ocean. If you dive down, you will find only a very slow movement. That slow movement does not create a change as such, but there is movement. As it does with the tree, the movement of the wind gives the waves and the ocean a different atmosphere, a different climate. That's why we insist that there is no change, but there is slight movement. And when you see that, you immediately have the answer to one of the most fundamental questions: is it natural to struggle?

The answer is yes and no. In Time Therapy we say that for those people who have a normal level of daily life, with all its related fears and anxieties, 70 to 80 percent of their struggle is to escape the fear of nothingness.

The fear of being nothing, the fear of ignoring your desires, the fear of doing wrong when you don't make an effort to work on yourself can become so huge that you escape through conflict. Conflict at least gives you a beautiful form of identification.

Have you observed how often in a relationship you go into conflict in a discussion? Simply out of fear of being the loser, of not being the one who is right. So yes, it's natural to struggle because one wants to escape the feeling of emptiness. But one can answer no to the question just as easily, because there is no need for struggle.

The sutra began by saying you are not your body, your body is not you, you are not the doer, but you are also not the enjoyer. You are pure awareness, the witness of all things. You are without expectation, free.

The expectation that you should be different is based on fear. Freedom, stillness is the end of expecting anything. Wherever you go, be happy. You are without expectation, you are free. The apple tree will live in misery if it expects to be full of apples all the time.

The apple tree that realizes that its being is as important as its fruit can stop the struggling. It can be in peace, it has freedom. Stop believing in the outside world's expectation that you must be a certain way. Radically ignore all expectations of yourself!

Ashtavakra says we are beings of our true nature, our Buddha nature, and so we are not born and don't have to fight to get back to that essence. We just have to learn to surf, to fly between these two worlds of the material and the spiritual. We have to use the intelligence of our beautiful minds, our egos, and the memory of the Buddha nature, flying and surfing between these two states without any fight or effort or struggle to become something other than who we are. There is nowhere to go. There is no need to become different, no need to change.

Imagine a beautiful blue sky. The color represents the climate; the space represents the atmosphere, the potential, the quality. The clouds flying by represent the mind. Why fight against the presence of clouds? Let them pass by! The sky is not going to go away because of the clouds. The color does not fade because of the presence of the clouds. All that happens is that sometimes you just see less of them, and at other times more. That's all! See this, says Ashtavakra, and be free.

Manuel Schoch is a gifted Swiss mystic, healer, therapist, and teacher. He was born in 1946 in Switzerland and from childhood has had the gift of being able to perceive energy fields. He has had various mystical experiences throughout his life.

He studied psychology in Switzerland and England, where he also refined his psychic skills. He worked as the youngest editor for the Swiss television network and as personnel manager of a large communication company.

After several years of studying with the Danish healer Bob Moore, Manuel started his own work as an energetic therapist in 1971. He was the co-founder of the Analytic Centre in Zurich and in 1974 he founded the HiHo-Collective, an anti-psychiatric institution which was well known in that time.

Manuel's style of teaching is both practical and very simple—ideally suited for twenty-first-century life. He teaches classes at the University of Zurich on "Bridging Science and Spirituality." Manuel developed Time Therapy, about which he gives international talks, workshops, and training programs, and he is the director of the Tune-In Centre for Time Therapy based in Zurich, London, and Athens, which he founded in 1984.

Manuel Schoch is married, has two sons and lives in Zurich.

SENTIENT PUBLICATIONS, LLC publishes books on cultural creativity, experimental education, transformative spirituality, holistic health, new science, ecology, and other topics, approached from an integral viewpoint. Our authors are intensely interested in exploring the nature of life from fresh perspectives, addressing life's great questions, and fostering the full expression of the human potential. Sentient Publications' books arise from the spirit of inquiry and the richness of the inherent dialogue between writer and reader.

Our Culture Tools series is designed to give social catalyzers and cultural entrepreneurs the essential information, technology, and inspiration to forge a sustainable, creative, and compassionate world.

We are very interested in hearing from our readers. To direct suggestions or comments to us, or to be added to our mailing list, please contact:

SENTIENT PUBLICATIONS
1113 Spruce Street
Boulder, CO 80302
303-443-2188
contact@sentientpublications.com
www.sentientpublications.com